Cameos of the
Salient Points Two
Ypres Sector 1914 - 1918

Ypres rises mystic in the sunset glow
The Menin Road winds where the waters flow
And those ever present ghosts that come and go
Speak to me softly
As the Flanders sun sinks low

Tony Spagnoly

Cameos of the Western Front
Salient Points Two
Ypres Sector 1914 -1918

by
Tony Spagnoly
and
Ted Smith

with an introduction by
Martin Middlebrook

LEO COOPER

By the same authors :
The Anatomy of a Raid
Australians at Celtic Wood, October 9th, 1917

Cameos of the Western Front
Salient Points
Ypres Sector 1914 - 1918

Cameos of the Western Front
A Walk Round Plugstreet
Ypres Sector 1914 - 1918

First Published in 1998 by
Leo Cooper/an imprint Pen & Sword Books Limited
47 Church Street
Barnsley
South Yorkshire S70 2AS

Front cover design by Ted Smith

A CIP catalogue record for this book is available
from the British Library

ISBN 0 85052 610 8

Typeset by IMCC Ltd. in 11/12 point Garamond Light.

Printed in Great Britain by
Redwood Books Ltd., Trowbridge, Wilts.

CONTENTS

PLATES

MAPS

DEDICATION

To Mary Ellen Freeman.

"Remembrance is the theme of her life."

"To live in the hearts
of those we leave behind
is not to die."

Headstone of Private Louis Rosenberg,
3rd Battalion Worcestershire Regiment,
killed in action 9th December, 1915, aged 27.
Prowse Point Military Cemetery
Warneton, Belgium

ACKNOWLEDGEMENTS

It is always the official institutions in these cases that merit a vote of thanks. Without the Commonwealth War Graves Commission, the Imperial War Museum the Public Record Office, and the Tank Museum at Bovington, modest military projects like this would never see the light of day. We are grateful for the patience and assistance of their respective staffs, for we know time is a valued commodity for them in this day and age when the interest in the years of 1914-1918 has been positively explosive!

Special thanks to Albert Ghekiere for his descriptions of the Institution Royale in the village of Messines as it was in 1914 and also his time spent in showing the crypt in the church as it is today. Again special thanks to Jack Patten for the amount of research he forwarded and the information taken from his private papers regarding the counter-attack of the 16th Battalion (The Canadian Scottish) on Kitchener's Wood. Jack is a serving officer with today's Canadian Scottish Regiment. Thanks are due to many other people, especially Mr & Mrs Joseph O'Donnell for permission to include the story of the O'Donnell twins (Joseph being the son of Jack O'Donnell), Mr P. W. Leigh for his permission to feature the exploits of his uncle Second-Lieutenant Hodson at Schuler Galleries, Kathie Willes and James Brazier for their assistance in bringing some professionalism to the proof reading, Colin Kilgour, always available to discuss the formation of the different Cameos, and Katie Nelson (now working in the Gulf) who was kind enough to type some of the early manuscripts.

Last but not least we must show gratitude to Corinne Smith who organised the typing of manuscripts, kept the budget down to reasonable proportions, organised computer supplies, and delivered and collected three children to and from their school while her husband made his frequent day trips to Ypres taking photographs, checking maps and generally enjoying himself.

Tony Spagnoly and Ted Smith, February 1998

PREFACE

A second edition of Salient Points is modestly presented in the hope that it will be enjoyed, if that be a suitable word to describe the reading of some poignant situations and the personalities involved in them.

This is not a guide-book nor an academic study of military actions and deeds which took place in some of the darkest, part-forgotten corners of the hallowed ground we collectively call the Immortal Salient.

What is this unseen emotional pull Ypres has on us, as year after year in increasing numbers, we succumb to this strange force that compels us to return?

Is it because we recognise perhaps that it was here in Flanders almost a century ago that the British professional army, once described as "a perfect thing apart", drew that historic line in the sand to defy the mightiest army that the world had seen, keeping faith with her smallest ally and, in so doing, left a generation of her finest in soldiers' graves around the little Flemish town of Ypres.

No matter how many times we stand at the Menin Gate Memorial to the Missing, winter or summer with attendant crowds or almost alone, the endless names carved upon this imposing edifice seem to send us a clear message not to forget. One of the age old truths of the church comes into its own, "In remembrance lies immortality'" and that surely must be correct.

The unique evening ceremony of *Last Post* strikes at the hardest heart as those powerful notes sail out on the evening air over the old salient. We cherish the hope that those lying in the multitude of military cemeteries surrounding Ypres hear and acknowledge this nightly mark of the towns people's respect.

It is difficult for the human mind to encompass all the pain and suffering that went on at Ypres, where every little hamlet entered the English military and domestic language as a byword for sacrifice, with perhaps Passchendaele the worst battlefield of all, way beyond our comprehension.

The poet, John Oxenham, after a visit here in 1917 wrote:

"The only way it seems to me to be able to view these fields of war and retain one's own faith and sanity, and the elemental belief in the sanity of one's fellows and essential goodness of God, is to regard them each in reverence as mighty altars on which for sake of a great ideal, mankind has proved itself equal to the most supreme of all sacrifices. Greater love hath no man than this."

This profound sentiment would surely have appealed to a widowed mother who, in 1920, travelled alone to Ypres on a cold icy day to stand at Hooge Crater Cemetery before the grave of her only son. She recalls: "I can write no more of your resting place, passionate weeping obliterates my every word. This piteous winter scene for me is Ypres. People coming after me in the endless years to come will see a tidy graveyard with crosses all in a row, and gently green undulating country, hummocky perhaps as uncultivated and uninhabited land often is, but they cannot, will not see what British soldiers fought for, lived in, and died in - tenaciously holding, sublimely, divinely for four long years!"

That grieving mother seems to have said it all. She and the great British armies of the time have now marched off the world stage, all we are asked in our turn, is to come and remember. A small price indeed.

Tony Spagnoly, 1998

INTRODUCTION

Why?

Why, more than 80 years after it ended, are more and more people visiting the battlefields of the First World War? Why are more and more books being published about that war? I have retired from my own writing career, but a study of my recent royalty returns shows that sales of my First World War books are actually increasing, despite one of them being nearly 30 years old, while sales on books of later events are diminishing. Why?

I think the answer lies in the fact that we are coasting gently (I hope) towards the end of the century – our century, the century in which we were all born and in which our forebears fought their wars and in which many died. I ask myself, how will history look back on our century and what will it judge the main features of it to have been?

I think that we can already see a sequence of events that will prove to be the century's landmarks: the First World War, the rise of Communism, a second global conflict, the Holocaust, the atomic age, the Cold War, the fall of Communism, the great leap forward in technology. And it was that first war, with its four-year-long stalemate-carnage on the Western Front that started that sequence and set the scene for what must have been seen as a momentous century. How, people will ask, could supposedly civilised nations send a whole generation of men into a conflict the outcome of which could only be decided when the supply of young men ran out? How could these soldiers endure their conditions so patiently – the survivors to return to a civilian world that barely comprehended what they had suffered, that often could not give them work, and then see their sons and daughters sent into another war because of the results of the shortsighted vindictiveness of some of the victorious politicians of the first war?

Yes, we look back in fascination on that land of trenches and graves. For the British it is an area so accessible that it can be visited on a day trip! Most of us have relatives buried 'out there'. I am lucky that my uncle, a Territorial platoon sergeant in the Lincolns, has a marked grave. We have a letter from a Belgian priest who buried this Catholic soldier "in the little cemetery near the field hospital" in October 1915. That was Remi Sidings Cemetery. Now it is Plot I of Lijssenthoek Military Cemetery and 10,000 further 'died of wounds' followed Uncle Andrew at that place of suffering.

I have known Tony Spagnoly for many years. Those who become active in battlefield affairs do so for many reasons. For Tony, I know his interest is for the purest of motives. As long as elderly veterans needed help with their visits, Tony was there to help. Now that phase is ending, he and his partner, Ted Smith, are performing the valuable task of setting down on paper for our enjoyment the exploits of some of the soldiers who died on the Ypres Salient. We remember the Somme where the Army of 1916 found its grave one summer and autumn, but the Salient is where the B.E.F. stood so doggedly for the whole four years of war and fought three major battles, where the tenure of the ground by British and Empire troops was so secure that every farm and nearly every lane and corner were given English names, the only sector of the Western Front to be so bestowed.

Thank you, Tony. Thank you, Ted. On behalf of Charles Bowes-Lyon, Lord Worsley, the Welch, the Welsh and the Worcesters, of young Condon and Lanoe Hawker, and all the others in your lovely little book, thank you for helping to keep their memory alive and to lead us to the scenes of their endeavours.

Martin Middlebrook, 1998

AUTHOR'S NOTE

"The Great War has resulted in the spilling of floods of ink as well as blood", so said Cyril Falls in his *War Books, A Critical Guide* – and he wrote that in 1930.

In recent years, the "spilling of floods of ink" has repeated itself, although the authors are of a different breed, most not having seen the "spilling of blood" and all putting pen to paper for different reasons. The 1914–18 conflict has been the inspiration for a proliferation of books, periodicals and other forms of literature. Likewise, it has been the subject of plays, enacted on stage and television, usually with a sound disregard for accuracy but a high level of romanticising about young, well educated, men who left their loved ones to fight the beastly Hun, and to 'go over the top' – all out of a deep sense of patriotism and anger at what the nasty Germans had done to poor little Belgium. Few cover the not so young and well educated, and not so poetic men; nor those who did not want to go to war, nor those who were only too happy to. These were the butcher, the baker, the candle-stick maker, as well as the inarticulate, the ignorant, the thief, the bully, the gambler, the cheat, the opportunist, the thug, the hooligan and the yobbo who served, but who did not go 'over the top' – but who fought just as bravely and died just as tragically.

There are also the documentaries, interviews, debates and poetry readings on radio and television – how many more times is the Great War to be represented by the same piece of footage showing men 'going over the top' even though the subject might be of actions where the fighting soldier did not 'go over the top', and had never even heard of a 'steel helmet' or a 'tin hat', let alone seen or worn one? The theme tune 'It's a long way to Tipperary' is also questionable when it comes to the songs, marching or otherwise, that the British soldier sang. Then there are the video cassettes and compact discs together with the screeds of material downloadable from the Internet. Schools are now treating the Great War as an historical subject, battlefield tours and battlefield visits are more popular than ever, and tour companies are opening up all over the place – on both sides of the Channel too! Associations, societies and clubs embracing the subject are flourishing, with the newsletters, bulletin-sheets and magazines they generate being distributed to an ever enthusiastic membership. 'Museums' of sorts are opening in all parts of the old battle areas and more and more hotels, guest houses and B&Bs are appearing to offer accommodation to the visiting traveller or 'Pilgrim'.

All this activity will ensure that those who gave their lives for King, country and otherwise are being remembered, and will continue to be remembered for the foreseeable future.

Much of this 'flooding of ink' is excellent, some of it bad, some of it academic and some of it verging on the pseudo-intellectual, written by those who read into events something which they want to see but which others will never see. A favourite input is criticism of the military leaders, generally written by those who have never made a serious decision in their lives, and who seem unable to try, or even want to try, to imagine the conditions, circumstances, political manoeuvrings or peer-pressures under which those leaders were trying to conduct a war,.

Most publications are well-constructed and presentable, a few are vague in objectives and amateurish in format. Some offer value-for-money - others are the closest you can get to an out-and-out rip-off,. yet others are produced as a labour of love. Most are well researched by established authors and historians. Many seem to be produced by frustrated authors and historians trying to prove they could have been what they are not. A good deal are written by those with little literary skill but with a deep interest, often spiritual, in the men who played their part in the Great War. Thankfully, many write on related specialist subjects and make available a good deal of worthwhile reference.

There are authors who take a superior stance, believing that the number of their books sold reflects on their ability as an author, ignoring the fact that without a professional distribution network their work would not be available for purchase anyway. As with the sale of any product, book sales tend to reflect the number of retail outlets where they can be bought and the amount of money spent in promoting them , and without enough of these two supporting factors, then bad luck! – try to get hold of a copy of *The Journals of Private Frazer*, just one example of an excellent book that didn't get the sort of back-up that would have put it on the shelves of popular bookshops. Others 'snipe' at the quality of the work of their contemporaries, and some frantically scan the work of others to find a mistake which will enable them to gleefully put critical pen to paper, but most, fortunately, just get on with the job of writing.

The results are published by organisations of various sorts, many by professionals in the printing and publishing industry, others by people who should never be allowed to put ink on paper and plenty by those who forget that someone, somewhere might want to read the piece they've printed and, in that scenario, presentation, format and type-character, all the subject of continual abuse, do play an important part.

One thing common to all these publications is that they are all subjected to the steely eye of the critic, many of whom haven't a clue as to what they are reading, but get a warm feeling from destructively criticising the works of others. Then, thankfully, there are those who offer constructive and objective criticism which does nothing but help the originator of the work in question.

At the end of the day it doesn't matter what critics choose to say as most of them don't know enough about the subject to qualify as critics – and in most cases have never written anything themselves, not that that is necessarily a qualification for a critic - but it helps. Nor does it matter who prints work for the public domain, although given a choice, which is rarely the case, a publisher with some knowledge of literature or book design, and an efficient distribution network, is desirable. Every page of every publication will serve to record something so that those who are interested can pick and choose, and make their own decisions on what is good or bad, right or wrong or useful or useless from the mass of Great War literature that will be available to them.

To those who have gleaned knowledge of the Great War over the years, on no matter what aspect, then share it! Get it down on paper! Do it for those who served and particularly for those who are lying in those many military cemeteries scattered throughout the world. Let the critics criticise, and never underestimate – or insult – the intelligence of the reader. The good stuff will last, the rest will bolster the coffers of the re-cycling industry.

The veterans of the Great War are passing-on daily and soon there will be none of them left with us. The battle areas are changing, and rapidly so in the case of Ypres and its surrounding villages. Those who have walked, researched and studied the battlefields before these changes, should consider themselves lucky, and particularly so if they had the privilege to have spent some time with a veteran of that war on those very battlefields. Those who have gathered collections of memoirs, recollections, regimental histories and other such publications that were readily available in the twenties and thirties, and who have chanced to come across trench maps, diaries and private papers of the period, are even luckier. These are precious items.

The men who fought and died in that war would have been puzzled, to say the least, at the reaction and profound effect it has had on the generations following, and particularly that generation who knew only of a Great Grandfather, or a Great Great Grandfather long since dead, or who have met with a 'vet.' whom they can't possibly imagine as a young man living and fighting in the most deplorable of conditions, and who had no idea he was fighting in the Second Battle of Ypres, the Messines Offensive or Passchendaele. He knew he was going into action but, in most cases had no idea what battle the action was part of, nor where, in a foreign countryside, it was enacted. That aside, it is these individuals and the actions they fought in that made up the armies and the battles that resulted in what was to be called "the war to end all wars" which then became the Great War and later, after the end of the Second World War, became the First World War.

It was the historians, military and otherwise, who developed the nomenclature, and who were given the tasks of recording events in an orderly manner. So we read of armies and corps, and divisions, brigades and battalions who took part in operations, offensives and battles on certain dates in certain years – but what we are really reading about are ordinary men who were identified by rank and number, fighting in muddy, foreign fields in little known actions, and who, when killed or wounded, became statistics in casualty lists of officers and other ranks, and their battalions became 'under strength' and were 'reinforced' with drafts or reserves.

All this terminology is taken for granted and it is difficult to imagine how war could be recorded otherwise, but it all still only refers to ordinary men taking part in actions that make up the armies and the great battles. Hopefully, we will never lose sight of this.

This book, as with those before it, and with those that will follow in the series, attempts to dissect the armies, the battles and the battlefields to bring them down to just that - the men, the actions and the places.

Ted Smith, February 1998

The Ypres Salient 1914–1918

The Pilgrim, when he visits Ypres and its now invisible Salient, will find it impossible to imagine how it was.

This modern, busy town and its surrounding villages embrace a community energetically employed in agriculture and light industry, seemingly unaware of the events of 1914-1918. But they are living and working in an area that is known to every regiment in the British army and which touched on the lives of hundreds of thousands of British families.

This is the Immortal Salient

Ypres itself was the centre of continuous battle from the first months of war until the end. It became a devastated ruin, without civilian habitation, but with an underground life of soldiery living like an army of rats in its cellars, only emerging at night to ply its trade of war.

The out-lying land to the north, east and south, called the Salient, was marked only by the ruins of villages, hamlets and farms, with odd English names as map references, and all surrounded by a barren featureless shell-holed morass with the occasional cluster of tree-stumps to mark a long-gone woodland.

These few square miles were a battlefield, a closely contained area ringed with guns, that lost all semblance of civilisation and became a bog in which a quarter of a million Allied soldiers died and hundreds and thousands suffered to ensure that the enemy should not pass.

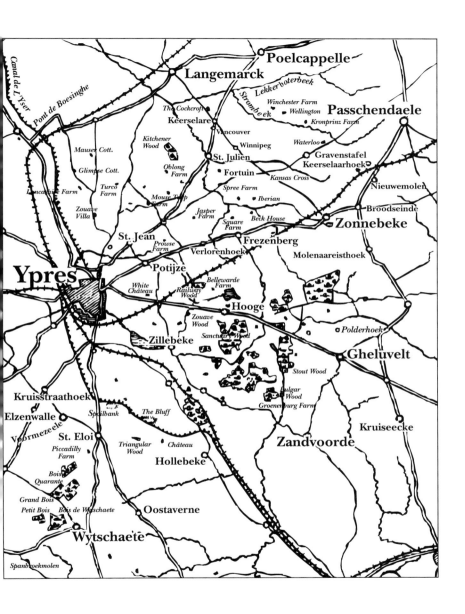

Canal de l'Yser

Pont de Boesinghe

Poelcappelle

Langemarck

Lekkerboterbeek

Strombeek

Winchester Farm

Wellington

Passchendaele

The Cockcroft

Keerselare

Kronprinz Farm

Vancouver

Kitchener Wood

Mauser Cott.

Winnipeg

Waterloo

St. Julien

Oblong Farm

Fortuin

Gravenstafel

Keerselaarhoek

Glimpse Cott.

Kansas Cross

Nieuwemolen

Lancashire Farm

Turco Farm

Spree Farm

Mouse Trap Farm

Iberian

Broodseinde

Zouave Villa

Jasper Farm

Square Farm

Beck House

Zonnebeke

St. Jean

Prowse Farm

Frezenberg

Verlorenhoek

Molenaareisthoek

Potijze

Ypres

White Château

Bellewarde Farm

Railway Wood

Hooge

Zouave Wood

Zillebeke

Sanctuary Wood

Polderhoek

Gheluvelt

Stout Wood

Kruisstraathoek

Bulgar Wood

Groenenburg Farm

Elzenwalle

Spoilbank

The Bluff

Kruiseecke

Voormezeele

St. Eloi

Triangular Wood

Château

Zandvoorde

Piccadilly Farm

Bois Quarante

Hollebeke

Grand Bois

Petit Bois

Bois de Wytschaete

Oostaverne

Wytschaete

Spanbroekmolen

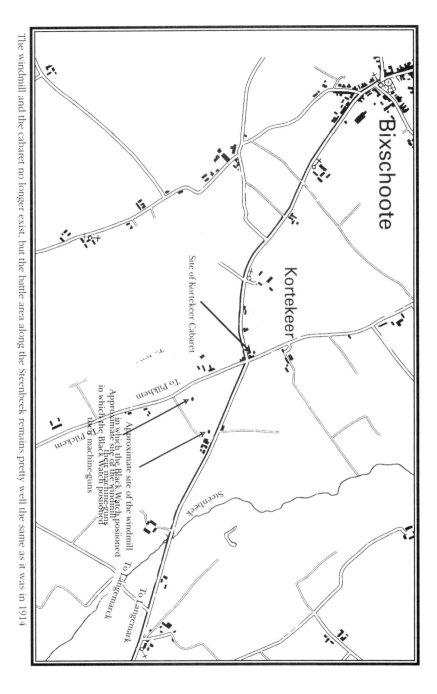

Bixschoote

Kortekeer

Site of Kortekeer Cabaret

Approximate site of the windmill
in which the Black Watch posioned
their machine-guns

Approximate site of the windmill
in which the Black Watch posioned
the machine-guns

To Pilkem

To Pilkem

Steenbeek

To Langemarck

To Langemarck

The windmill and the cabaret no longer exist, but the battle area along the Steenbeek remains pretty well the same as it was in 1914

1

THE BLACK WATCH AT YPRES
Lieutenant C Bowes-Lyon, Kortekeer Cabaret and Black Watch Corner
Langemarck- October 1914

W*ithout labour there is no coming to rest, nor without fighting can victory be obtained.* So is stated in the opening pages of the official history of The Black Watch Regiment dedicated to the men of the Regular, Territorial and Service battalions who laid down their lives during the Great War of 1914 - 1918.

Imposing statistics are also presented to endorse the claim that, in no part of the British Empire, was there a more hearty response to the call for men than in Scotland. No less than twenty-five battalions of the Black Watch were raised to serve on every battle front from the Aisne in northern France to Kut-al-Amara on the road to Baghdad. In dispensing their duty, 69 battle honours were gained during this terrible war adding to the 28 honours already awarded since 1725 when the colours of the regiment were first raised. Nearly 30,000 men enlisted during the Great War years, and 8,000 were fated to lay down their lives. It would be a tragic loss for this gallant formation, and few could have had any conception of what lay ahead when the first companies left Southampton on the steamship *Italian Prince* on 13th August 1914 to arrive the next day at the French port of Le Havre.

Sadly, this loss of men would be an average rate to be endured by many regiments in the British Army before the guns would fall silent four years later.

One interesting ingredient of the Black Watch make-up as it embarked for overseas service was that it was 92% Scottish born.

This reflected the reliance of the British Army on Scotland as a prime area for recruitment - good use of the inherent martial capacity of the Scots, evident since they stopped the Imperial Legions of Caesar at Hadrian's Wall.

The 1st Battalion, 1st Brigade, 1st Division, played its full part in all the early battles in which the British Expeditionary Force was involved. They were with it at Mons, on the long gruelling retreat south and then on to the Marne and the Aisne.

A junior officer wounded during the Aisne fighting was 23-year-old Lieutenant Charles Bowes-Lyon a member of an aristocratic Scottish lowland family, and cousin to a future Queen, the much loved Queen Mother of today. By the time Lieutenant Bowes-Lyon recovered from his wound, the battalion was *en route* to Ypres, involved in what was to become known as the "race to the sea" where both armies leap-frogged each other's positions in a desperate bid not to be out-flanked.

The long trek north from the Aisne uplands had taken them almost a month, taking part in minor activities in the La Bassée sector on their way. They rested at Hazebrouck, marched on to Poperinghe on 20th October, then across country by the many by-roads to Elverdinghe and Boesinghe on the Yser Canal.

In Flanders the Black Watch were to engage in warfare totally different frrom what they had experienced to date. Mobile and open combat to which they had become familiar in the south was out, and the fighting was of a restricted and more intense nature. The German army, frustrated in its aims several times already, were now applying its full strength in attempting to break the thin British defensive line around Ypres, to gain the Channel ports and divide the Allied command.

On the 21st October, whilst the battalion rested in the area of Pilckem, the 1st Brigade, and specifically the Cameron Highlanders acting as flank guard to French units, were beginning to feel the pressure being applied by the Germans advancing in force from the north-east.

They had posted a strong guard at Kortekeer Cabaret, a small inn at the crossroads a mile north of Pilckem on the Langemarck-

Bixschoote road, critical because its position opened the routes to Langemarck, Bixschoote and Pilckem.

Early on 22nd October, the enemy attacked, and the Highlanders and a small detail of Coldstream Guards assisting them, were overrun, with both units sustaining heavy casualties.

The 1st Battalion Black Watch, leaving its 'C' Company as a small defensive picket about Pilckem, set off with its remaining three companies to help restore the situation at the crossroads - Lieutenant Bowes-Lyon was in 'A' Company under the command of Captain Edward F. M. Urquhart, a 37-year-old clergyman's son from Edinburgh.

Around 6 p.m., 'A', 'B' and 'C' Companies, supported by dismounted French cyclists, pushed on to the main Langemarck road and took positions along the Steenbeek. Their machine guns, under Lieutenant F. Chalmers, being set-up in the ruins of a windmill situated 200-300 metres east of the crossroads.[1] From here they inflicted heavy casualties on the German troops. The enemy, ever mindful of their attack plan being delayed by the handful of obstinate Scots ahead, intensified fire, and soon the windmill became a roaring inferno. After three to four hours of non-stop fighting, both sides settled down to maintain a watchful gaze on each other.

The enemy had taken possession of Kortekeer Cabaret but the next day the Divisional 2nd Brigade counter-attacked and re-took it. The Black Watch were able to act as spectators to this counter-attack from their fire-pits along the Steenbeek. In the action, 60 Cameron Highlanders were released from the cabaret having been held as prisoners for the night.

During all this activity the windmill ruins continued to burn, providing a dramatic backdrop to events. By midnight on 23rd October, the British position around the Kortekeer Cabaret had been fully restored. After midnight the enemy attacked in force, bearing down on the small garrison around the cabaret in packed formations, blowing bugles and trumpets and singing. The attack was kept at bay by the defenders with heavy losses taken by both sides.[2]

After repeated counter-attacks, all of which were repulsed, the Germans withdrew, their efforts expended. They would lick their wounds for six months until April 1915 when in the Second Battle of Ypres, they would test the resolve of the defenders of Ypres once more with their new weapon, chlorine gas.

The Black Watch, had played their part well and, on 24th October, they were relieved by French troops. They left the sector of the burning cabaret and ruined, smoking windmill behind, pausing only to salvage equipment and bury their dead. They then headed south to lend assistance to their hard-pressed colleagues warding-off massed attacks around the Menin Road where the First Battle of Ypres was reaching its critical stage. In mid-November 1914, in the peaceful surroundings of Westoutre in West Flanders, the 1st Brigade concentrated on recovering its strength, taking in much needed reinforcements from infantry depots. The Black Watch welcomed nearly 300 new men to its ranks, replacing those who fell in the actions at Langemarck, and the Menin Road.

When the Black Watch left the Kortekeer sector, moving back towards Pilckem they had carried with them the bodies of Lieutenant Bowes-Lyon and Captain Urquhart.

The battalion-history names only these two officers as having fallen in the action, fierce and intense as it was. No details exist to denote how they met their fate, but as 'A' Company, to which they both belonged, was part of the screen along the Steenbeek river, just yards out into the salient before the Kortekeer Cabaret, they were obviously victims of one of the many German attacks.

Captain Urquhart and Lieutenant Bowes-Lyon were buried together in the corner of the little churchyard at Boesinghe. A strange move when the remainder of the action's casualties were left three kilometres away at Kortekeer Cabaret.

They were left in this tranquil spot until, in the mid-1920s at the express wish of the Bowes-Lyon family, the Lieutenant was re-buried at New Irish Farm Cemetery, St Jean.[3]

Captain Urquhart was left where he was first buried in 1914. A sad little tale which will explain to many casual visitors why this gallant officer lies alone.

The 1st Battalion made their mark again in the sector in November of the same year when its 'C' Company manned a defence section at the south-west corner of Polygon wood. Commanded by Lieutenant Anderson it held back the advance of the Prussian Guard on a small woodland called Nonne Bosschen.

On 11th November, following the Kaiser's order to break through at all costs, the Prussian Guard attacked in force, driving back 'A' and 'D' companies of the Battalion and broke through the line. 'C' Company, in its support position, split the attackers into small parties with tactically applied gunfire, causing the momentum to be taken out of their attack. This corner, so gallantly defended by Lieutenant Anderson and his company, was the first instance in the war of a position being wired-in as a 'strongpoint'. From the 11th November action this little corner of the battle area became known as Black Watch Corner, a fitting tribute to the Black Watch and the men who served in the regiment.

Notes.

1. The windmill, which was not replaced after the war, stood several hundred metres back from the cabaret on the right of the road to Langemarck with the Steenbeek winding its way along the left hand side of the road.

2. The German casualties from the Langemarck action were concentrated in the large German cemetery sited near the village. Graves were not finally concentrated here until the mid-1950s.

3. A letter from the Commonwealth War Graves Commission to Ted Smith dated 16th November 1995 states:

"According to our records, Lieutenant C. L. C. Bowes-Lyon and Captain E. F M. Urquhart, both of the Black Watch, were killed on 23 October 1914 and buried together in a joint grave in Boesinghe churchyard. Many graves were lost as a result of heavy shelling from which the churchyard subsequently suffered, but the remains of these two officers were identified. After the war the next of kin were asked if they would prefer their remains to be re-buried in the same churchyard, or transferred to the nearest war cemetery. Captain Urquhart's next of kin chose the former option, and Lieutenant Bowes-Lyon's the latter. The register of the Boesinghe Churchyard was published in 1929 after the transfer of Lieutenant Bowes-Lyon's grave to New Irish Farm Cemetery, and therefore includes only Captain Urquhart's entry. "

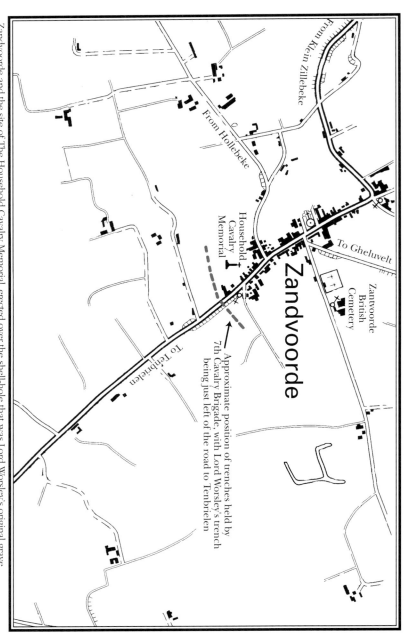

Zandvoorde and the site of The Household Cavalry Memorial, erected over the shell-hole that was Lord Worsley's original grave

From Klein Zillebeke

From Hollebeke

Household
Cavalry
Memorial

To Gheluvelt

Zandvoorde
British
Cemetery

Zandvoorde

To Tenbrielen

Approximate position of trenches held by
7th Cavalry Brigade, with Lord Worsley's trench
being just left of the road to Tenbrielen

6

2
LORD WORSLEY, ROYAL HORSE GUARDS, ZANDVOORDE
Ypres, 30th October 1914

IN OCTOBER 1914 THE VILLAGE OF ZANDVOORDE on a ridge south-east of Ypres was one of the points being probed by the German 39th Division in a bid to detect any weakness in the British line. It was a critical sector of the line with dismounted cavalry, part of the 7th Cavalry Brigade, facing the enemy in front of the village and the 1st Battalion Royal Welsh Fusiliers, 7th Division on their left flank. The Germans were keen to break through here as the road to Zillebeke and its surrounding woodland would open the way for them to move on Ypres itself.

On a grassy knoll before the village, the Household Cavalry, in their new role as infantry, were positioned in trenches just south of the Zandvoorde-Tenbrielen Road. These rudimentary trenches, badly sited on the downward slopes of the knoll, were in full view of an approaching enemy. The left flank of the brigade, in trenches close by the road, comprised 'C' Squadron of the 1st Life Guards commanded by Captain, the Lord Hugh Grosvenor. The squadron had a commanding view of all that was likely to approach them, but this was counter-balanced by the fact that they were themselves, on the open high ground, exposed to enemy eyes. In the centre of 'C' Squadron's trenches was a young aristocrat, 27-year-old Lord Charles Sackville Pelham Worsley, a machine-gun officer of the Royal Horse Guards. He had already spent seven days and nights in the trenches, and, when the Life Guards had relieved the Royal Horse Guards in this part of the front, he was detailed to stay behind with his gun team, the Life

Guards having one of their guns out of action.

He had prepared his section for action, but neither he, nor anyone else, was prepared for the onslaught that would thunder down on the position the next morning, 30th October.

Lord Grosvenor was aware of the danger presented by his squadron's isolated position and contacted brigade headquarters asking for artillery fire to protect his flanks, but at 6 a.m. on the 30th, before this support could be effected, the Germans opened a devastating bombardment on the position, dedicating most of their 260 guns to the same. This was followed at 7.30 a.m. by the German 39th Division plus three Jäger Battalions hurling themselves against the pathetically thin line of the Household Cavalry stretched along the knoll. The attack was a resounding success for the enemy who took complete control of the Zandvoorde Ridge from where they proceeded to lay down enfilade fire on the right flank of the 7th Division, obliterating the 1st Battalion Royal Welsh Fusiliers who had been fighting-off the massed infantry attacks themselves.

Orders were issued to withdraw to a second line and by 10 a.m. the British in the sector had retired in good order, except for the two squadrons on the left flank, including Worsley's machine-gun section. The order did not reach these two squadrons and they suffered almost total extinction. About ten men got back, but all the remaining officers and other ranks were listed as missing, Lord Grosvenor and Lord Worsley amongst them.[1] Worsley was last seen directing his gun as shell-fire exploded around him, the mound of enemy corpses before his position giving mute testimony to his team's action during the morning. As the survivors made their way to the shelter of the woods at Klein Zillebeke, his gun was heard chattering its defiance before an eery silence embraced the Zandvoorde knoll.

The British cavalrymen had vacated the area, leaving their dead comrades on a now German-occupied sector of a Flanders battlefield, but it had been a galling experience for the enemy who had been held back by so few British defenders. The British had not been able to halt the German move towards Ypres in this sector, but the cost to the enemy had been heavy, and valuable time was gained for British Command.

News of Lord Worsley being missing was sent to Haig at 1st Corps Headquarters near Hooge, who was distressed to hear it as his family was linked to Worsley's in marriage. Lord Worsley was officially declared missing on 7th November and, only in January 1915, was it announced officially that he had been killed.

A German officer, Oberleutnant Freiherr von Prankh, interested to know who had served the British machine-guns, found the body of a British officer lying in a trench. On examination he found that the dead officer was a cavalryman and an English Lord. He arranged a burial party, and left instructions for the dead man's personal effects to be collected. These he intended to pass on to the authorities to return to the next of kin, but he was himself killed a few days later and Lord Worsley's personal effects were lost forever. In July 1924, his identity disc was found attached to a death list of a German Sanitary Company with a statement that no further effects had been handed in.[2] The disc was eventually passed on to Worsley's family who, in the meantime, had managed to obtain from the War Office, via diplomatic channels in Holland and the American Embassy in Berlin, a detailed plan of where he had been buried.

A family friend, Colonel A. W. James M.C., was given a copy of the burial plan by Worsley's mother, Lady Yarborough. He was determined to find the grave, and although a first attempt was a failure, a second, made in December 1918, proved successful. He had secured the service of a 10th Hussar veteran who knew the area well, having fought within a mile of Zandvoorde in October 1914. On reaching the crossroads south of the ruins of Zandvoorde, they took bearings from the sketch, the accuracy of which enabled them to walk straight to the exact spot of the grave.

A rough wooden marker cross had been erected by the German burial party on Worsley's grave, where it remained for the rest of the war. They noted that the upright of the marker was there, the cross piece having fallen off, or maybe having been knocked off, during the shelling the area had been subjected to.

That any of it survived at all is nothing short of a miracle as this exposed slope was subjected to heavy Allied shelling until the Germans were able to move closer to Ypres in November 1914.

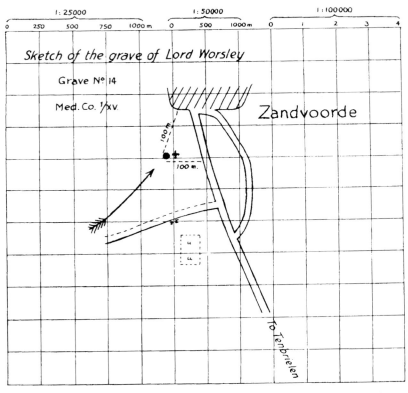

Sketch of the grave of Lord Worsley

Grave Nº 14

Med. Co. 1/xv.

Zandvoorde

100 m.

To Tenbrielen

The English officer was lying in the hole made by a heavy howitzer shell, and was buried therein, together with other fallen Englishmen. The spot could not be specially distinguished as at the time the hostile artillery swept this very spot as soon as anybody showed himself.

Now located through the Medical Corps 1st Co. 15th Army Corps.

PLACE.   DATE.

Copy.   25/2.

WASSERBURG.

The foregoing sketch is of the grave of Lord Worsley, Royal Horse Guards.

Fallen and buried on the 30/10/14.

Capt. Thiesen can no longer remember exactly whether he sent the disc of the English officer to the regiment or to the Brigade direct.

In the regiment nothing is known.   *(Signed)* BAUERNSTEIN.

The map passed by the German authorities to Lord Worsley's family

It was standing on what had once been a shell-hole, now a tangle of rough, overgrown vegetation. There were no other graves in the immediate vicinity and Colonel James rightly concluded that this was the spot beneath which Lord Worsley lay in his soldier grave. He marked the spot with rough blocks of stone in case the old cross upright should fall down and returned to the village where he was staying, and commissioned a simple wooden cross to be made inscribed with the words "Lord Worsley, R.H.G., Oct. 30th, 1914."

His next visit to the grave, he made with Sackville Pelham, Lord Worsley's brother, in January 1919. The weather was cold and depressing and, when they reached Ypres, snow was falling heavily, blanketing the immediate countryside to a depth of three inches. They collected the newly-made cross at the ramparts in Ypres and proceeded as far as the ruined village of Gheluvelt from where they made their way cross-country, taking with them five German prisoners-of-war and an escort, the prisoners being detailed to carry the cross and various tools.

On arrival at the grave they found the old marker upright still in place. They started to place the new cross and, after digging down about six inches, found the original cross piece. When the new cross was in place they took with them the old upright and cross piece, together with a cutting from a battered osier fence growing near the grave. The upright and cross piece, now put together as a cross, hangs above Lord Worsley's sword in Brocklesby Church in Licolnshire, and the osier cuttings were struck at Herstmonceux Castle, Colonel James' father's home in Sussex, and several of the plants were later to adorn the grounds of Worsley's family estate in Brocklesby.

Lady Worsley was aware of all this activity and, after months of correspondence with relevant government agencies, purchased the piece of ground in Flanders in which her late husband rested.

In the summer of 1921, the concentrating of the war graves within the Ypres Salient was in full flow. More than four hundred plots in Belgium had been ceded in perpetuity to Britain and, as Lord Worsley's grave was in an isolated position with no firm

Colonel James' replacement cross, in place over Lord Worsley's grave

arrangement to begin a local burial plot, a decision was made to remove his body for re-burial in Military Extension No. 291 of the Town Cemetery of Ypres, just outside the Menin Gate, a short distance along the road to Zonnebeke. The decision was conveyed to Lord and Lady Yarborough and Lady Worsley who gave their agreement. A family friend, the Reverend R. S. Swann-Mason, an ex-naval chaplain, consented to represent the family at the exhumation. On 7th September 1921, he reached Ypres and attended the site with a Captain Ryan, O. C. Exhumation Military Authority to verify the position of the grave. The exhumation took place the following day, with the body being found five feet below the cross erected by Colonel James and Sackville Pelham.

That it was the body of the Lord Worsley there was no doubt as parts of the uniform markings, the body dimensions and a gold-filled tooth clearly confirmed it to be such. His remains were placed in a coffin of rough timber which was then covered with a Union Jack and taken, with its cross, to the morgue at Austral Camp, a hutment area just outside the town gates at Ypres.

The burial service took place at 10 a.m., 9th September with a burial party of four officers carrying the Union Jack - Major Allen of the Australian contingent stationed at Ypres, Captain Ryan, head of the exhumation camp, Captain C. W. Renshaw, Lieutenant Summers and six private soldiers making up the carrying party, with the Reverend Swann-Mason representing the family.

After final prayers, the grave was filled and the cross from Zandvoorde placed upon it, where it remained until 1923 when the War Graves Commission headstone replaced it. This cross was returned to the family and now hangs opposite the original German grave marker and Lord Worsley's sword.

His headstone features the words:

Lieutenant
Lord Worsley
Royal Horse Guards
Zandvoorde
30th October 1914, age 27
He died fighting for God and Right and Liberty,
And such a death is immortality

The Household Cavalry Memorial was erected on the land that Lady Worsley bought at Zandvoorde, the site of her husband's original grave. The memorial was unveiled on 4th May 1924 by the Earl and Countess Haig.

Opening his address Field-Marshal Haig said:

It is my privilege today to attend the unveiling of this memorial not only as Colonel of one of the three famous regiments whose gallantry it commemorates, but as the representative of His Majesty the King, in whose service their gallant deeds were done.

So there it stands today, the memorial a mute witness on its hallowed ground, once the shell-hole grave of an English Lord, to heroic deeds of so long ago, not only to those of Lord Worsley, but to all cavalrymen who having unsaddled their mounts fought dismounted, proving their worth by standing firm, and many times, fighting to the last man.

Notes.

1. Lord Grosvenor Hugh Williams aged 36, 1st Life Guards was first buried at Zandvoorde in 1914, but his grave was lost in later shelling. He is remembered on the Menin Gate Memorial to the Missing, Ypres. It was common knowledge that the Germans were familiar with the names of many English notables who served in the Guards and the Household Cavalry. It was likely that they knew Lord Grosvenor was in the trenches at Zandvoorde and that he was the brother of the Duke of Westminster. Likewise, it is probable that they knew that Lieutenant Hon. Gerald Ward of the same regiment, and also in the Zandvoorde trenches, was a brother of the Earl of Dudley. The fact that Lord Worsley's body was the only one with a marked grave must be accredited to Oberleutnant von Prankh's interest in who manned the British machine-guns on the day. The fact the the Oberleutnant was also of cavalry training and of the German aristocracy would have influenced him in his decision to arrange for the burial of Lord Worsley.

2. Worsley's identity disc was handed in by a Hauptman Fischer of the German Infantry Regiment 5/171. He was killed later in the war.

An early photograph of the Household Cavalry Memorial at Zandvoorde. Post-war development in the area has relegated its position to an area behind the back gardens of local dwellings

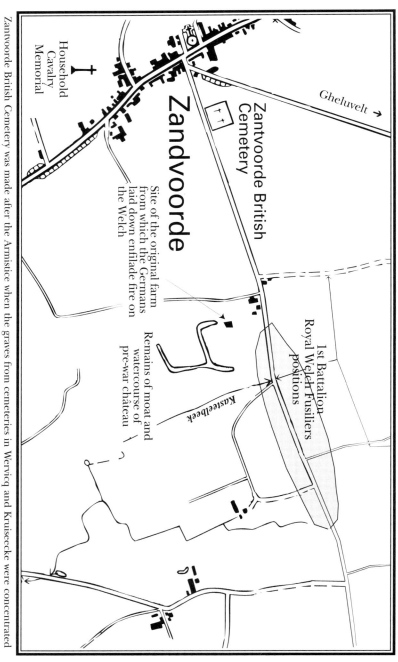

Zandvoorde

Household
Cavalry
Memorial

Zantvoorde British
Cemetery

Gheluvelt →

Site of the original farm
from which the Germans
laid down enfilade fire on
the Welch

Remains of moat and
watercourse of
pre-war château

Kasteelbeek

1st Battalion
Royal Welch Fusiliers
positions

Zantvoorde British Cemetery was made after the Armistice when the graves from cemeteries in Wervicq and Kruiseccke were concentrated there. The fallen of the 1st Royal Welch Fusiliers are believed to be among the 1,135 unidentified who are buried in the cemetery

3
1ST ROYAL WELCH FUSILIERS AT ZANDVOORDE
30th October, 1914

A T THE END OF OCTOBER 1914, hard-pressed units of the 7th Division, British Expeditionary Force were inching back along the Menin Road to Ypres as German pressure brought the First Battle of Ypres to its final crescendo.[1] From Langemarck, north of Ypres, to the Messines Ridge in the south, the battles raged, with the main weight of the enemy employed abreast the Menin Road. It was here they hoped that cracks would appear in the thin line of British troops.

The 7th Division had only arrived in Belgium at the end of the first week of October and had spent the better part of the second week marching backwards and forwards across the north Flanders plains as rearguard to withdrawing French and Belgian troops after the fall of Antwerp.[2] The 15th October saw it arrive in Ypres before forming-up on the 18th for what was planned to be a decisive attack to capture the German-held town of Menin, east of Ypres.

The early stages of the battle, the attacks on Dadizeele, Gheluwe and Zandvoorde, were progressing favourably when, in the early afternoon, the Germans mounted a fierce attack on the division's left flank forcing the British infantry to hold its advance and eventually to dig-in. On the 19th, they were forced to retire to positions they had held two days before and the Germans were throwing all they had against what was now a thin, stretched line of defenders.

The desperate battle for the town of Ypres, later to be called The First Battle of Ypres, had begun.

The whole of the British Army was now on the defensive and its infantry was falling back all along the line. Zonnebeke to the north had fallen and intense pressure was being directed by the enemy on either side of the Menin Road, the road that would take them through to Ypres.

The 7th Division with the 7th Cavalry Brigade had taken tactical positions on the sloping ground around Zandvoorde and the Gheluvelt Ridge and were fighting desperately to maintain them. Both positions offered the occupiers invaluable observation points over the low ground leading to Menin, and the Germans were as keen to take them as the British were to hold them. The fighting was fierce and ground was reluctantly conceded to overwhelming numbers of the enemy. At Zandvoorde the Germans were verging on the frenzied in their determined efforts to break through, but squadrons of the 7th Cavalry Brigade, acting as infantry, and men of the 1st Battalion Royal Welch Fusiliers of the 22nd Infantry Brigade, barred the way. The cavalry lay in front of the village whilst the Welshmen, commanded by Lieutenant-Colonel Henry Cadogan were on their immediate left, straddling the road leading due west out of Zandvoorde.

The Royal Welch Fusiliers had taken heavy casualties earlier in the battles fought around Zonnebeke and the Broodseinde crossroads when, after they went into reserve behind Polygon Wood on 21st October, their roll-call showed 345 men killed, wounded or missing leaving the battalion with an effective fighting strength of only 212. Now on the night of 29th October, with that strength raised to over 400, they found themselves in rudimentary trenches on the extreme right of the line held by the 7th Division flanked by the dismounted cavalrymen of the 1st and 2nd Life Guards.

The night passed quietly, but early on the morning of 30th October the Germans, who had effected their reliefs, registered their guns and having taken up their battle positions during the night, advanced in strength following a heavy bombardment laid down by their artillery.[3]

The 1st Battalion took-up position in slit-trenches on a forward slope of a slight rise in the land east of Zandvoorde where it became party to a situation which would seal its fate in this desperate struggle at the gates of Ypres. The Cavalry Corps was holding a wide front with the 1st and 2nd Life Guards to the right of the Fusiliers. The heavy bombardment and sheer weight of numbers of the advancing German infantry caused orders to be issued for a retreat to the support line approximately 1,200 yards to the rear. This order never reached the Royal Welch, and the Life Guards conducted an orderly withdrawal unknowingly leaving their compatriots with an open right-flank. Nevertheless, even under such disadvantageous conditions, the Welsh riflemen continued to mow down the advancing lines of units of the 39th German Division, inflicting heavy losses.

The Germans, fully exploiting the advantage of the opening left by the Life Guards' retirement, quickly moved their field-guns into the village of Zandvoorde and immediately brought down vicious enfilade fire on the 1st Battalion's trenches. They had also occupied a large farmhouse about thirty yards to the right of the Welsh trenches and from here were firing at point-blank range into the battalion. As if this wasn't enough, numbers of their troops, using hedgerows as cover, worked their way to the rear of the battalion who now, with field-guns to their right, attacking infantry to their front and snipers working to their right and rear, found themselves completely cut-off. Section after section was eliminated and every effort made by reinforcements to reach them was thwarted by a triumphant enemy as it pounded the desperately fighting Welshmen almost to extinction. The action continued throughout the day and it was not until the evening that those of the battalion who could, received orders to retire, their job done and vital time gained, leaving a supporting unit to take the strain 1,000 yards in the rear.

Mustering at Hooge the next morning, only 90 men answered the roll call. Lieutenant-Colonel Cadogan, seven officers and 320 other ranks were either killed wounded or missing. This gallant battalion had temporarily ceased to exist as an effective fighting unit. Lieutenant-Colonel Cadogan had left the trenches to help his adjutant Captain Dooner who had been seen to fall after having delivered orders to a section of the battalion. Cadogan himself was killed and now lies between his batman, Private Davies, and Captain Dooner in Hooge Crater Military Cemetery.[4]

The Battalion diary for that fateful day of 30th October 1914, reads:

The enemy attacked the trenches of the Battalion at daybreak, and enemy, because of Cavalry on the right giving way, enabled to enfilade the trenches.

The exact nature of casualties that day are unknown but the following officers and about 320 N.C.O.s and men were found to be missing - Lieut. Colonel H. O. S. Cadogan, Lieut. B. C. H. Poole, 2 Lieut. Egerton, 2 Lieut. Woodhouse 1R.W.F.; Capt. E. E. Banner, Capt. W. Vincent, 3 D.C.L.I.; Capt. J. H. Disney, 3 Essex; Lieut. C.V. Edge, 2 D.C.L.I.; Capt. H. Robertson, R.A.M.C.

No accurate information is obtainable regarding this action, but it is hoped that this record will be verified and completed with further details on the return to duty of those officers who were actually engaged and now prisoners of war.

No officer remained after the 30th October and the party which survived on that date (approximately 86 other ranks) were attached to the 2/Queens.

Second-Lieutenant Woodhouse, one of the officers of the regiment who was wounded and taken prisoner, did document an account on the day's engagement on his return to duty:

30th October.- We were holding a line about three-quarters of a mile long, A Company on the right, then B, D and C on the left. Battalion H.Q. was in a dugout about 600 yards to the rear. The trenches were not well sighted for a field of fire. So far as I know, no one was on our right; some 'Blues' were supposed to be there, but I did not see them. It was foggy in the early morning, so that the Germans could not shell us much, which was lucky, as they had two batteries on Zandvoorde Ridge. About 8 a.m. the shelling increased, and we saw large numbers of Germans advancing down a slope about 1,500 yards to our front. Also I believe large numbers were seen coming round our exposed right flank. The batteries on the ridge were now firing point-blank into our trenches, so that it was difficult to see what was happening, and the rifle fire also increased from our right rear. No orders received, so it was thought best to stay where we were, and about midday the whole battalion was either killed, wounded or taken prisoner.

Casualties: Colonel Cadogan, Dooner, Egerton, and an officer of the Cornwalls killed, self wounded and prisoner, Poole, Evans, and Barrow (Cornwalls) prisoners. During that day, or the next Barker, who was doing Staff-Captain, was killed.[5] I was taken to a dressing-station in Zandvoorde and patched up.

The Germans were suffering heavily from our shell fire and were unable to use the road. I saw some of their guns get stuck in the mud behind the village. I do not know what the strength of the Germans was, but I believe it was at least a regiment (Hanoverians). I was struck with the fact that they had 'Gibraltar' on their shoulders.

The devastated 1st Battalion, later to gain immortality in the writings of Siegfried Sassoon and Robert Graves who joined the Royal Welch Fusiliers the following year, was regenerated and served splendidly until the Armistice in November 1918. Its colours display the battle honour "Zandvoorde 1914" with justifiable pride.

Today the actual battleground, apart from a few new buildings, road improvements and, of course, The Household Cavalry Memorial and Zantvoorde British Cemetery remains pretty well the same as it was in October 1914.[6] The farmhouse which was so prominent during the battle was destroyed in later fighting and was rebuilt on the corner edging the main Zandvoorde-Comines road and a side road.[7]

Notes:

1. The 7th Division was made up of the 20th Brigade – 1st Grenadier Guards, 2nd Scots Guards, 2nd Gordon Highlanders and 2nd Border Regiment; the 21st Brigade – 2nd Royal Scots Fusiliers, 2nd Wiltshire Regiment, 2nd Yorkshire Regiment and 2nd Bedfordshire Regiment; the 22nd Brigade – 1st Royal Welch Fusiliers, 1st South Staffordshire Regiment, 2nd Warwickshire Regiment and 2nd Queen's Royal West Surrey Regiment; the Northumberland Hussars Yeomanry; a Brigade Division Royal Field Artillery; four 4.7 guns; and detachments of Royal Engineers and R.A.M.C.

2. The Division was originally designed to relieve Antwerp but it arrived in Belgium too late (6/7th October 1914). It was employed instead to cover the

retirement of the Belgian Army. In doing this the Division covered 160 miles in marching to and fro across northern Flanders. It was the first of the British troops to enter Ypres and was ordered to hold the line before the town until the other six divisions of the B.E.F could be brought up from the Aisne. Ordered to hold on at all costs, it was in continual action from the 15th to the 31st October. It went into action with a strength of 18,000 with no reserves or supports. It held a single line covering eight miles of front with only 18 field pieces and four 4.7's and a minimum of ammunition, but it held on against some 340,000 Germans, with guns in proportion. On the 31st the Division was withdrawn only 2,000 strong - and these practically only transport and supply.

3. Between the 24th and 30th October, the German Supreme Command had formed an Army under General Fabeck to bolster their attacks which so far had failed to pierce the British line. This Army was to attack the Messines-Hollebeke-Zandvoorde line on 30th October supported by 260 heavy guns - such a large artillery formation had never been heard of, and certainly not used before, in this early part of the Great War.

4. Lt-Colonel Cadogan, his batman Pte No. 10936 Allen Davies and his Capt.-Adjutant lie together in Hooge Crater Cemetery. The cemetery register records: Pte. Allen Davies, Plot IX, row L, grave 10, Lt-Col. H.O.S. Cadogan, Grave 11 and Capt. A. E. Claude Toke Dooner, Adjt. Grave 12.

5. Captain R. V. Barker was killed the next day, 31st October while acting as Staff-Captain to the 22nd Brigade. At the end of the battle the brigade, under Brigadier-General Lawford, was left with four combatant regimental officers and some 700 men, little more than a battalion in strength. The Brigadier-General's son, Peter, was a Hollywood movie star in the 1930s. He died in the 1950s.

6. Only one member of the 1st Battalion is noted in the register of the cemetery. Of its 1,583 total, 1,135 are unidentified. It is believed that, amongst these, are the bulk of those Fusiliers who died on 30th Oct. 1914.

7. The resident farmer when ploughing his land often had problems with the footings of the original farm. All traces of these old footings have since been removed.

The 1st Battalion Royal Welch Fusiliers were sited either side of this winding road during the action of 31st October 1914. The village of Zandvoorde from where the 1st Battalion were shelled by German artillery can been seen on the rise in the background. The farm from which they took such devastating enfilade fire from the German infantry stood to the left of the farm seen on the bend of the road.

23

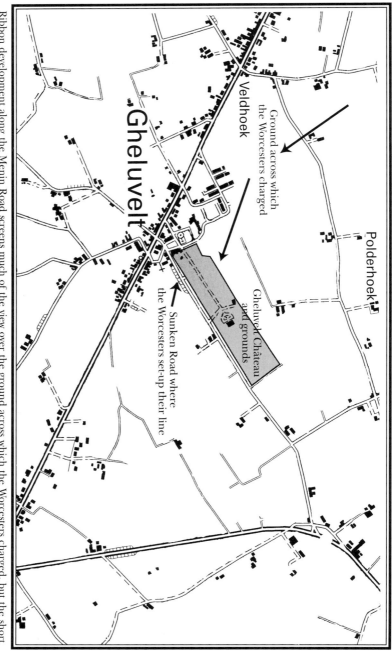

Ground across which the Worcesters charged

Veldhoek

Polderhoek

Gheluvelt Château and grounds

Sunken Road where the Worcesters set-up their line

Gheluvelt

Ribbon development along the Menin Road screens much of the view over the ground across which the Worcesters charged, but the short drive to Polderhoek is worth the efort to get a Worcesters'-eye-view of it

4

THE WORCESTERS AND THE WELSH AT GHELUVELT
Ypres, 31st October 1914

IN OCTOBER 1914, THE GERMAN ARMIES were committed to defeating the British Expeditionary Force and occupying the Channel ports, a situation the British were determined to deny them. The opposing forces were locked in battle along a line sweeping south from a point between Broodseinde and Keiberg, north-east of Ypres, down to Kruiseecke, south-east of the town, and then south-westward to Le Gheer on the Franco–Belgian border. There was but one day in that traumatic October when the Germans had the opportunity, the resources, the incentive and the place to break the British line and achieve their ultimate desire.

That day was 31st October; the resources were their three Army Corps - 120,000 fresh troops against a battle-weary British army of, at best, 25,000; the incentive was the Kaiser himself, headquartered just behind the front to view the battle, having issued an order to break the British line, no matter what the cost; and the place - the village of Gheluvelt sitting on the Menin Road five miles south-east of Ypres, the old capital of West Flanders - and to take Ypres was to open the way to the Channel ports.

The British Commander, Sir John French, had abandoned earlier attempts to capture the German occupied town of Menin, and was not aware of the build-up of enemy troops on the Menin front, nor of the Kaiser's wish to break through at this point. The British were defending a front from the village of Zandvoorde, south of the Menin Road, to the Zonnebeke–Moorslede road, just west of Zonnebeke, to the north-west. The 7th Division manned a front from Zandvoorde north-east to the Ypres–Menin road, the

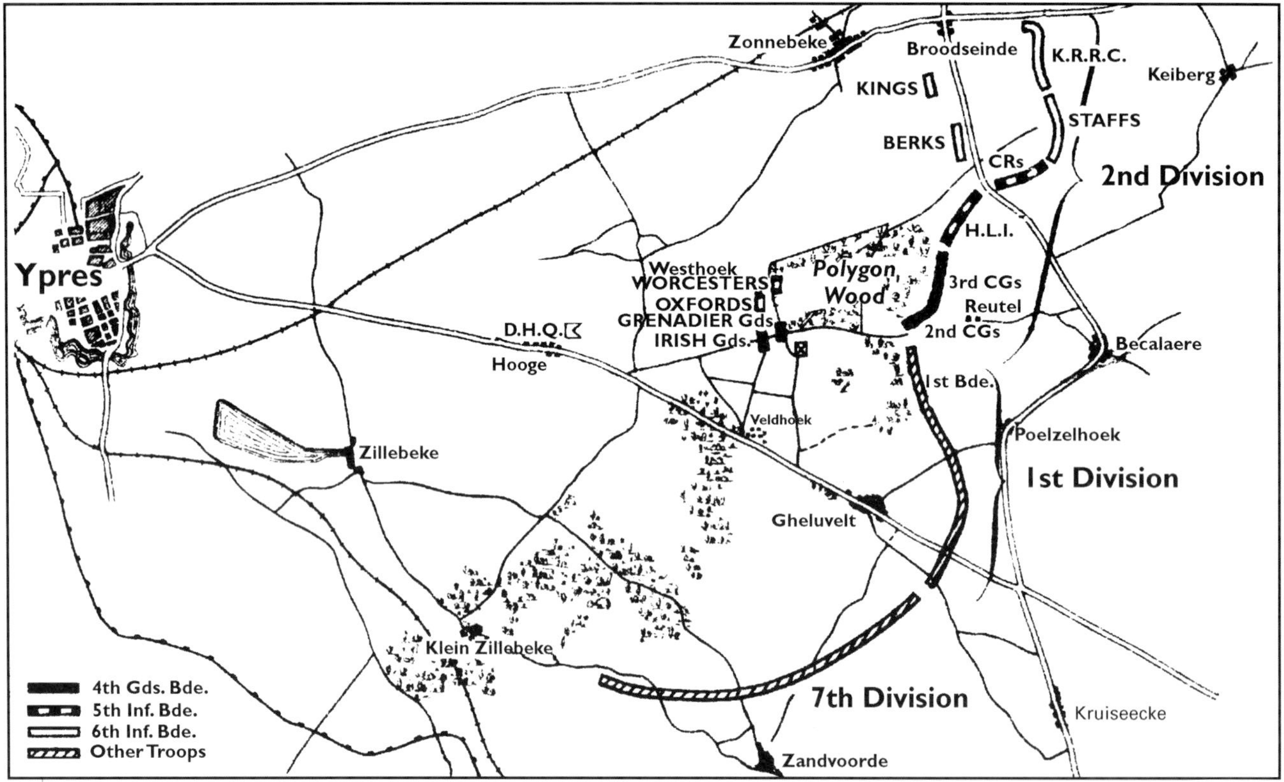

The situation, 31st October 1914

Legend:
- 4th Gds. Bde.
- 5th Inf. Bde.
- 6th Inf. Bde.
- Other Troops

Ypres

Zillebeke

Klein Zillabeke

Hooge

D.H.Q.

Zandvoorde

7th Division

Gheluvelt

Veldhoek

Westhoek
WORCESTERS
OXFORDS
GRENADIER Gds.
IRISH Gds.

Polygon
Wood

3rd CGs
Reutel
2nd CGs

1st Bde.

1st Division

Kruiseecke

Poelzelhoek

Becalaere

H.L.I.

CRs

BERKS

KINGS

STAFFS

K.R.R.C.

Keiberg

Broodseinde

Zonnebeke

2nd Division

1st Division from this point to just west of Reutel, and the 2nd Division from Reutel to the Zonnebeke-Moorslede road.

Gheluvelt on its plateau west of the Kruiseecke–Poelzelhoek, Ypres–Menin crossroads, was an obstacle to the German advance on Ypres. An important height for observation, it was manned by the 1st Battalion, South Wales Borderers, the 2nd Battalion, Welch Regiment and the 1st Battalion, Queen's (Royal West Surrey Regiment) of the 1st Division. - about 2,000 men. They were outnumbered by about four to one.[1]

East of the crossroads was the junction of the German XXVIIth and XVth Corps, the latter part of the newly formed Army Group Fabeck which had moved to Gheluvelt especially for the occasion.

On 29th October the Kaiser had arrived to watch the forthcoming actions and, in dense fog which didn't help his observation, a whole German Army Corps attacked, marching through the crossroads, and breaking the extremity of the British front where the 1st and 7th Divisions met. The attack was repulsed by units of these two divisions as the fog lifted, but they took extremely heavy casualties in the doing. At the end of a day of attack and counter-attack and continuous enemy bombardment, the enemy had gained no more than 500 yards of trenches at the crossroads. They renewed their attacks the next day, and Zandvoorde to the south fell to the them, an important gain of high ground - and a critical loss of the same for the British. The line north of the Ypres–Comines canal to Gheluvelt was now under threat, with a jubilant enemy preparing to attack in force.

On the 31st, Gheluvelt came under bombardment from the east, supported from the south by the newly established artillery in Zandvoorde. Then followed an attack, with the troops cheering and singing, knowing their beloved Kaiser was there to watch their onslaught - but again they were repulsed. In keeping with the Kaiser's wish to break the British line at all costs, they attacked again, with the same result. Another barrage, another attack, and then again, and yet again - each time with fresh troops from their massive force mustered in the Menin sector - and each time they were beaten-off by the outnumbered and battle-scarred British.

Taking the brunt of the attack in the village were men of the 2nd Welch Regiment and the 1st South Wales Borderers. Their defensive efforts, and the price to the Germans following their Kaiser's wish, was reflected in the heaps of his dead and wounded soldiers cluttering the approaches to the village.

During these attacks, German command noted that rifle-fire to their south was closer, indicating that the British were falling back, and that the breakthrough might be made south-east of them.

Realising that if the village wasn't taken quickly others would claim the honours of victory and, mindful that the Kaiser had his beady eyes on them, they attacked again, but this time to the left of the road and village, outflanking the nearest regiment. They cut-off the 1st Battalion, Queen's (Royal West Surrey Regiment) who fought to the death, most falling where they stood. A few fought their way out and back to what little was left of the British reserve line. The 2nd Battalion Welch Regiment to the left of the Queen's, were literally blown out of their trenches by artillery fire. Forced to retire, they left part of the battalion to support the right flank of the South Wales Borderers in the village, but these were quickly overcome by the German infantry now storming the village.

The Germans decided to open the gap between the 1st and 7th Divisions by using the same manoeuvre against the 2nd Battalion, Royal Scots of the 7th. Again it worked, the Scots fought to a standstill. but now the 7th Division's flank was open and the 1st Division was pulling back. Gheluvelt had been taken, the road to Ypres was open - the Kaiser thinking it just a matter of time before his victorious armies paraded in the market-square of Ypres.

North of Gheluvelt the line held. Artillery fire had forced the two right companies of the South Wales Borderers to retire back through the Gheluvelt Château grounds, with the rest of the battalion, less exposed to the artillery, holding its line alongside the Scots Guards. The Welshmen counter-attacked immediately, smashed their way back into the grounds seeing-off the victorious Germans with the bayonet and point-blank rifle fire.

They re-formed just outside the eastern walls of the château, a little in rear-right of the rest of the battalion. Here they held, with the Scots Guards on their left, but with their right flank open, no supports and a very aggressive German Army in front of them. The British situation was desperate. Their line was broken. Repeated attacks had been resisted by units reduced to less than half strength. With no reinforcements and little artillery support, the position was critical. Sir Douglas Haig, from his base in Hooge with Commander-in-Chief, Sir John French, decided to retreat. The British were on the run - and the Germans were on their way to the Channel ports via Ypres.

The 1st Division was ordered to retire to a line between Klein Zillebeke and Frezenberg to cover the retreat of the rest of the force. If this line was broken then another, a mile back, crossing the Menin Road at Hell Fire Corner was to be held at all costs.

Then something happened which changed the direction of the war. A runner brought news that the 1st Division was reforming its line and the enemy was retiring. The South Wales Borderers had stood firm when the enemy took Gheluvelt and the British line caved. They carried on firing and held their ground against all-comers. When orders were issued to retreat they stayed where they were - but they needed reinforcements if they were to hold the flank, giving the 1st Division the chance to reform.

They were in trouble, cut-off from the rest of the line and with anyone trying to reach them having to cover ground being drenched with shell and shrapnel fire. The reinforcements, should they come, would carry the fate of the gallant Welshmen on their shoulders - as well as that of the British in Flanders.

Brigadier-General FitzClarence commanding the 1st (Guards) Brigade, had sent reserves to fill the gap in the broken line but without success. He rode-off to his divisional headquarters to report and was informed of the presence of the 2nd Worcesters in the south-west corner of Polygon Wood, north of Gheluvelt, about 600 of them acting as 2nd Divisional reserve, currently taking a well-earned rest from the previous weeks of hard fighting.

Although belonging to another division, Major E. B. Hankey, their commanding officer, made arrangements to put them at the disposal of FitzClarence who, having determined the line of attack using the battered village church as a landmark, ordered them: "To advance without delay and deliver a counter-attack with the utmost vigour against the enemy who had taken possession of Gheluvelt, and to re-establish our line there.[3]

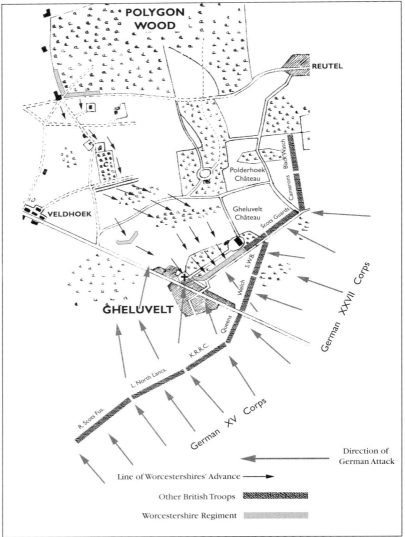

Counter-attack by the 2nd Battalion, Worcestershire Regiment

On receipt of the order, Major Hankey sent-out a party of six scouts to reconnoitre the ground and cut any wire that would cause obstacles. Most of them died in the attempt. He dispatched his 'A' Company to occupy a trench 400 yards north-west of Gheluvelt between the wood and the village, to support the Borderers and to check any advance of the enemy. This move in itself was a feat of tremendous daring - one company advancing against a German army to hold a trench-line - but they did it!

The rest of the battalion deployed in Polderhoek Wood, west of Polderhoek Château about 600 yards south-east of Polygon Wood. Extra ammunition was issued, back-packs discarded and bayonets fixed. In two lines they set-off, passing through the wounded of the 1st Division regiments moving to the rear. For the first half-mile they were in the cover of sparse woodland, but always under shrapnel-fire. Everywhere there were signs of retreat with the only movement forward being these men of the Worcesters. The following 1,000 yards was open country with no cover at all. It was crowded with the dead and the retiring wounded, and under heavy artillery fire. Major Hankey decided to cover this ground in one long rush and, nothing daunted, the Worcesters stormed forward. When the running wave of bayonets was seen by enemy observers they brought down a deluge of shells and, in the first 200 yards, 100 men fell. The rest kept going, reaching the fences enclosing the château grounds. These they cleared, quickly routing the German infantry in the château and its grounds, and actually in rear of the South Wales Borderers. The Worcesters were surprised to see the Welshmen still holding on. Major Hankey went to their commanding officer and found him to be an old friend, Colonel H. E. Burleigh Leach. The second-in-command, Major A. J. Reddie was a brother of Major J. M. Reddie of the Worcesters. "My God, fancy seeing you here." said Major Hankey, with the Colonel replying: "Thank God you have come".

General FitzClarence, who had gone with Major Hankey to the deployment area, remained there to watch the attack. On seeing its success, he galloped back to Polygon Wood reporting to the 1st Division: "It's all right, my line still holds north of the village."

31

The Charge of the Worcesters by Gilbert Holiday

The Worcesters set up their line in the sunken road fringing the edge of the boundary of the château grounds, forming up on the right of the 1st South Wales Borderers who were more than a little overjoyed to see them. About 300 yards to their front was a small wood filled with Germans who were laying down fire wherever, and on whoever, they wanted. This didn't suite the mood of the Worcesters at the time, and they gave vent to their anger by subjecting the wood and its occupants to devastating rifle-fire, clearing the threat it represented for good. Nevertheless, they were in a situation that was anything but safe, with enfilade fire from Saxons of the German 242nd Regiment sweeping their right flank from the ruined village. Having just suffered a harrowing experience getting to the road, and having put paid to the occupants of the wood, the Worcesters were not prepared to put up with any more. They stormed the village and cleared it at the point of the bayonet, causing the Germans to think twice before attempting more sorties on this flank. The Worcesters could not occupy the centre of the village due to both British and German bombardments, but they held the line to the crossroads east of it. After dark the British Command withdrew and consolidated a new line about 600 yards west of the village and, with it, the only sure chance the Kaiser's armies had of reaching the Channel ports was gone forever.

An extract from Sir John French's despatch, describing the action of 31st October states:

> Meantime, on the Menin Road, a counter-attack delivered by the left of the 1st Division and the right of the 2nd Division against the right flank of the German line was completely successful, and by 2.30 p.m. Gheluvelt had been retaken with the bayonet, the 2nd Worcestershire Regiment being to the fore in this, admirably supported by the 42nd Brigade Royal Field Artillery ... I was present with Sir Douglas Haig at Hooge between 2 and 3 o'clock on this day, when the 1st Division was retiring. I regard it as the most critical moment in the whole of this great battle. The rally of the 1st Division and the capture of the village of Gheluvelt at such time was fraught with momentous consequences. If any one unit can be singled out for special praise, it is the Worcestershires.

The 2nd Worcestershire's diary covering their action, reported the battalion's tremendous achievement as, simply:

31st October 1914. Position of front line of 1st Division driven in. Battalion ordered to deliver a counter attack and endeavour to re-occupy trenches of South Wales Borderers and Welsh Regiment. Battalion advanced under very heavy shell-fire and suffered heavy casualties. Drove the Germans out of the grounds of the Château at GHELUVELT and got touch (sic) with the South Wales Borderers. No reinforcements arriving, a general withdrawal of the line was ordered; this commenced Company by Company at about 6 pm. Battalion then occupied a line of trenches immediately North of VELDHOEK facing East. On the front line being taken up by 1st Brigade, the Battalion was withdrawn to the reserve at the N.W. Corner of a large wood. (Wounded: Captain Gascoyne-Williams, Lieutenants E. C. R. Hudson and E. A. Haskett-Smith. Total casualties about 130).*

* The Official History of the War sets the casualties as three officers and 189 other ranks, killed wounded or missing

So that was that! The line had held and the Kaiser's armies were committed to another four years of warfare.

The 2nd Battalion Worcestershire Regiment deserved every bit of the praise showered upon them at the time. Because of their courageous charge the battle at Gheluvelt was turned from disaster into victory, but what of the South Wales Borderers? Without their courage, tenacity and fighting abilities, not to mention their down-right stubbornness, the Germans would have forged through the gap and would surely have driven through Ypres and onward toward Calais, and then what? Who knows? In the Kaiser's words, his armies "would have carried out an attack of vital importance to the successful issue of the war."

The Kaiser had had his day ruined. His wish had been dashed by a thin line of tired, battle-worn, men in mud-plastered uniforms, but determined men with rifles, bayonets, plenty of ammunition and a grim desire to use all three. They would not be taken lightly, nor would they consider defeat. They chose to stand firm and fight it out, and by so doing set the example for the many thousands of British troops who were to take part in other battles in the long years of the Great War to come.

These were the qualities of the men who fought the desperate fight at Gheluvelt, and it was the Welsh and the Worcesters who demonstrated these qualities on behalf of all the units that fought what was to become known as the Battle of Gheluvelt in the First Battle of Ypres.

The memorials to the 2nd Worcesters and the 1st South Wales Borderers in a lane opposite the Gheluvelt village square, to the right of the road running down to the sunken road where the Worcesters set up their line following their charge. The Worcesters' memorial was originally unveiled on the wall of a cottage built in the village by the Homes for Disabled Belgian Soldiers, on 31st October 1925. The care of the memorial was entrusted to the occupant, the 760th Belgian soldier listed for such a dwelling, a Corporal van Laer who was disabled by wounds he received at Passchendaele on 8th April 1918.

Notes:

1. Two battalions of the 105th Infantry Regiment, 1st Battalion 143rd Regiment, a strong mixed detachment from the 54th Reserve Division, mainly from the 245th Reserve Regiment and 26th Reserve Jäger Battalion; the 99th Infantry Regiment - in all about eight battalions.

2. The formation was made up of XVth Corps, commanded by General von Deimling, 2nd Bavarian Corps and the 26th Württemberg Infantry Division. The 6th Bavarian Reserve Division, which had arrived at Dadizeele a few days earlier, was also in the line.

3. Brig.-Gen. FitzClarence who issued the order to counter-attack was killed on 12th November while leading the 1st Irish Guards in a counter-attack against the Germans in Polygon Wood. A farm he used as H.Q. just south of Glencorse Wood was named after him. His body was never recovered and he is commemorated on the Menin Gate Memorial to the Missing in Ypres. He was awarded his V.C. for conspicuous bravery in action on two occasions during the Boer War whilst a Captain in the Royal Fusiliers.

4. Hooge Château was the H.Q. of Field Marshal Haig. He shared it with the 1st Division H.Q., until he decided to move to White Château, further down the Menin Road toward Ypres, to enable General Munroe and the 2nd Division H.Q. to take up residence with the 1st Division.

At 12.45 on the 31st, as the Worcesters' counter-attack was getting under way, Maj.-Gen. Lomax (1st Division) and Gen. Munroe (2nd Division), with their respective staffs, held a meeting at the Château H.Q. High explosive shells disrupted the meeting causing a catastrophe. Maj.-Gen. Lomax was wounded and died some months later in England. Col. E. W. Kerr, G.S.O.I. 1st Division; Lieut.-Col. A. J. Percival, G.S.0.2 2nd Division; Major G. Paley, G.S. 1st Division; Capt. R. Ommaney, G.S.0.3 2nd Division; Capt. F. M. Chenevix-Trench, Brig.-Maj. R.G.A., 2nd Division and Lieut.-Col. R. H. H. Boys, D.S.O., C.R.E, 2nd Division, were killed on the spot. Lieut. H. M. Robertson, A.D.C., R.A., 2nd Division and Major I. W. Forsett were wounded. Lieut. R. Giffard, A.D.C. to Gen. Lomax and Lieut. G. P. Sheddon were wounded and later died of their wounds. Gen. Munroe was badly stunned, but uninjured, Col. Wingham G.S.O.I. 2nd Division being the only officer unwounded. There were seven killed amongst the N.C.O.s and O.R.s attached to the H.Q. The five officers killed on the spot are buried in a single row of seven graves, Plot III, Row AA, in the Ypres Town Cemetery Extension, flanked by Gunner J. Marchant of the 35th Heavy Battery R.G.A. and Pte. J. Barton, 1st Battalion Leinster Regt. Lieut.'s Giffard and Sheddon are buried just inside the southern boundary wall of the cemetery, on the outside edge of the path ringing the civilian burial plots, in Row E.1 Grave 12 and Row E.2 Grave 2 respectively.

5. Gheluvelt was not re-captured as such. It was cleared of the enemy but on the evening of the 31st the right of the 1st Division withdrew to join with the left of the 7th Division which had lost ground during the day. Gheluvelt was re-occupied by the Germans who stayed there until 1918.

The eastern edge of the Gheluvelt Château grounds and the sunken road used by the Worcesters to form their line following their bayonet charge

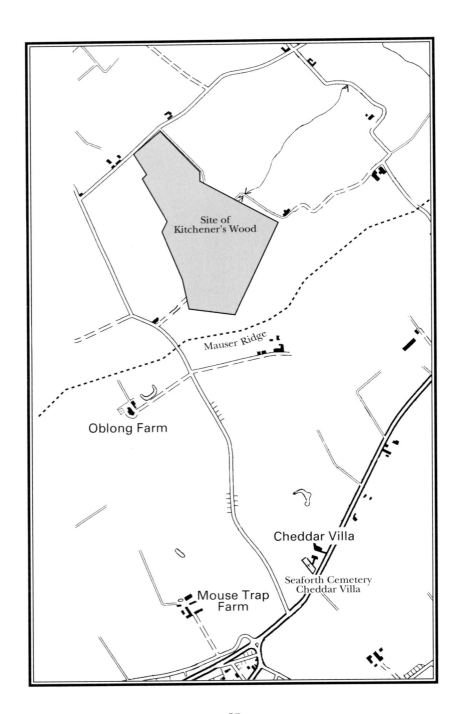

Site of
Kitchener's Wood

Mauser Ridge

Oblong Farm

Cheddar Villa

Seaforth Cemetery
Cheddar Villa

Mouse Trap
Farm

5

THE YOUNGEST SOLDIER
John Condon, 2nd Royal Irish Regiment
Mouse Trap Ridge, May 1915

IN THE GREAT WAR OF 1914–1918, teenagers from all over Britain and the Empire, as it was then, rallied in their thousands to fight for the Mother Country. Boy service had been a tradition in Britain's armed forces for several hundred years, from the drummer boys who accompanied the Duke of Marlborough in his European campaigns, to the 'powder monkeys' running along the gun decks to service Admiral Nelson's fleet. In the Royal Navy of Queen Victoria's day, 14-year-old boys had put to sea with the fleet. Following this tradition, Boy Seaman Jack Cornwell, at 16 years old earned a place in history as one of the youngest holders of the Victoria Cross, Britain's supreme award for gallantry. This was at the Battle of Jutland in 1916 when, aboard the cruiser *H.M.S. Chester*, he stood on the open deck beside his lifeless gun, amid the dead and wounded, awaiting orders from bridge control to 'lay' the gun. Orders that never came! He died of his wounds shortly afterwards.[1]

Although service at sea for youngsters was common practice, the Army barred anyone younger than 18 years from participating in action, and if a lad did slip through the net, as so many did, parents could reclaim their erring off-spring as their permission was required before the aspiring boy soldier could take the King's Shilling. It was expected that many youngsters would try to break the age barrier before the baleful eye of the recruiting sergeant, especially during the early years of the Great War, when patriotic enthusiasm was at its peak. Many did, and served proudly in the front line.

The identity of Britain's youngest fallen soldier exercised minds over a long period. Eventually it was established that, as far as official records would show, and as far as ever might be proven, Private John Condon of the Royal Irish Regiment was the youngest. He died the day before the Second Battle of Ypres closed-down in May 1915, barely 14 years of age.

Several other claimants arose at one time or another, but these were eventually discounted in favour of John Condon. They had included Rifleman Reuben Barnett of the Rifle Brigade, killed in action at Ploegsteert Wood in 1914, aged 15 years and buried at Rifle House Cemetery; Rifleman Valentine Studwick, also of the Rifle Brigade, also 15 years old when he died in 1915, now buried in Essex Farm Cemetery, Ypres, and Private Alphonse Carroll of the 22nd Battalion Canadian Infantry, who is buried at Wancourt near Arras on the old Hindenburg Line. Carroll was killed during the final British offensive in 1918, and was long thought to be 14 years old at the time of his death, before investigations established his true age as 18 years old. There may be others in soldier graves who warrant consideration, but they are unknown to us.

John Condon was born of John and Mary Condon in the parish of Trinity, County Waterford, Ireland in June 1901, but no birth certificate exists to give the exact day. From all accounts he was a lad with an ambition to be a soldier, a desire that would be accorded him sooner than he could have hoped. He must have looked older than his years as, in 1913, he joined the local county militia giving his age as 16 years old, the peacetime minimum.

When war broke out in 1914 he was caught up in the general rush to enlist. Irishmen from both sides of the religious divide flocked to the colours. There were those in the southern counties who must have been bemused by the eagerness to do this, considering the prevailing agitation for Home Rule, an issue that had threatened to spill over into civil war in 1914. Irishmen have worn the King's uniform for centuries, and Irish regiments have as proud a history of service as any from the British Isles. Victory in the European war offered the prospect of some form of home rule being granted by a grateful government, and this fired the imagination of many Irishmen. Whatever the reasons, recruiting sergeants on the Emerald Isle were as busy as those across the water and Irish regiments earned their laurels in all theatres of war. John Condon would play his full part. He progressed from the militia into the local infantry unit, the 3rd (Service) Battalion Royal Irish Regiment, then at its home depot in Clonmel on the county border with Tipperary. John remained there in the early days of the conflict whilst the 1st and 2nd Battalions prepared themselves for war.

The 1st was destined to head east where they joined the 10th Irish Division in its operations in Salonika, Egypt, and later in Palestine. The 2nd Battalion embarked to France in November 1914 before moving to the Ploegsteert sector in Belgium to join the 12th Brigade, 4th Division.

The Second Battle of Ypres had begun in April 1915 with the first use of poison gas by the Germans north of the city. The gas attack caused a serious break in the Allied line as French Colonial troops broke contact under its effects, and began to flood back east over the Yser Canal, causing a critical gap in the line which the Germans would do their best to exploit. That they were unable to was mostly due to the gallant defence of the St. Julien area by the 1st Canadian Division whose historic stand was to win them undying glory. The British rushed up all available units, working feverishly to support the Canadians and help plug the gaps. One of these units was the 4th Division. All through late April and into early May the fighting was fierce, and became deadlocked on those gentle folds and ridges around those fortress farms which were a feature of this part of the Flemish landscape. Every move by the enemy was blocked by the resourceful British defenders, with attack after attack thrown back by a tenuous line who took heavy casualties, but never broke.

The 12th Brigade, 4th Division, rushed up from Ploegsteert and held the tip of the salient jutting out into German lines near St. Julien, with the 2nd Royal Irish in position near Mouse Trap Farm and its attendant ridge.[2] The fighting had been intense for several weeks, and the battered farm complex had changed hands several times since the early days of the battle.

A draft from Clonmel, with John Condon amongst it, entered the fray to make up the 2nd Battalion's strength. With his family unaware of his whereabouts, young John was about to earn himself a strange immortality - but one chapter of his life was closed - he would never see Ireland's shores again!

Towards the end of the month the enemy made a last effort to break the wavering line. May 24th, Whit Monday, dawned, a fine day in prospect for the enemy's final assaults. Mouse Trap Farm and the ridge it sat on was subjected to prolonged heavy shelling and saturated with gas.[3] The defenders made ready for another test of fortitude and, peering through the smoke and haze, awaited the enemy. After this shower of steel, the Battle of Bellewaarde Ridge, as it became known, began as four German divisions hurled themselves against three defending British brigades, from Hooge in the south to Mauser Ridge near Mouse Trap Farm in the north. The fighting was fierce. Every advantage in yards gained by the German infantry was countered by the stubborn defenders, with the Irish regiments of 12th Brigade covering themselves with glory on Mouse Trap Ridge. The 2nd Royal Dublin Fusiliers lost over 500 on the 24th May, making a regimental total in recent weeks of 1,200, for, in far-off Gallipoli, the 1st Dublins had lost 700 men.

These figures left both regular battalions of the Dublin Fusiliers virtually destroyed. Meanwhile, their compatriots of the 2nd Battalion Royal Irish Regiment, with John Condon in their ranks, were also making a gallant stand. Only yards from the enemy and taking the brunt of a gas cloud enveloping the area, they were pushed back. One company, unable to repel the attackers, lost the ruins of Mouse Trap Farm. This German triumph was short-lived however as an immediate counter-attack threw them from the farm before they had time to settle.

Combat was savage, but the line held and by nightfall the Germans were spent. Troops of the German 51st Reserve Division had had enough. No local advantage was developed and due to fatigue and shortage of ammunition, orders were received from

German Fourth Army H.Q. that no more operations be undertaken, and the fighting died down.

Both sides needed the breather and a chance to take stock. The Second battle of Ypres was over and the German Army had failed yet again to take Ypres. It had hammered at a rock-like defence, and this time had incurred casualties of 860 officers and over 34,000 other ranks. The line stayed in the position left at the end of 24th May, 1915 until the Third Battle of Ypres began two years later on 31st July, 1917.

The 2nd Battalion Royal Irish Regiment had lost its commanding officer, 16 officers and 378 other ranks killed, wounded and missing. John Condon was one of them. The lad from County Waterford, so determined to join the forces of the Crown, had found himself a soldier's grave in Flanders, and it was only on the day he died that his family discovered that he was included in a draft that had been destined for the front. His body was buried on the battlefield but, when hostilities ended, he was exhumed and re-buried at Poelcappelle.[4] Providence must have smiled on his original grave as the area was subjected to persistent gunfire by both sides. Visitors to the Poelcappelle British Cemetery north of Ypres, where young John Condon lies, will note that the cemetery register, as well as his headstone at Plot LVI, Row E, Grave 10, gives his age as 14 years - not quite the truth, as befits the young Private who fell a month short of his 14th birthday.

Notes

1. Jack Cornwell V.C. died of wounds on 2nd June 1916 in a hospital at Grimsby, two days after the Battle of Jutland. He is buried in Manor Park Cemetery, Essex.

2. Mouse Trap Farm is now a working farm. It was called Shell Trap Farm during the early Ypres fighting, but was later changed for reasons of morale.

3. Mouse Trap and Mauser Ridges remain much as they were, and the view of the battlefield of 24th May 1915 is unimpeded.

4. Private John Condon is buried in Plot LIV., Row E., Grave 10 at Poelcapelle British Cemetery, Belgium.

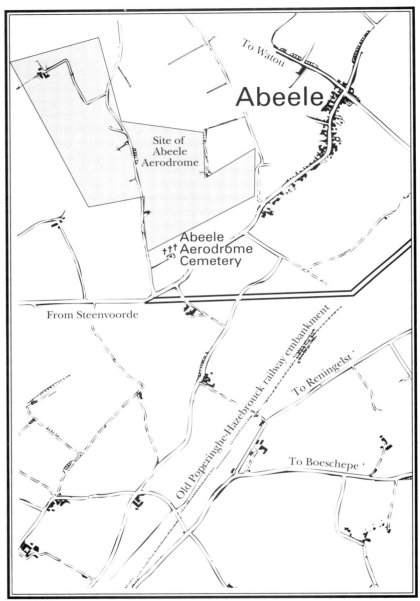

The old road through Abeele and its frontier-post into Belgium is no longer used for the purpose of entering the country. Steenvoorde is now the frontier-crossing and the road from there to Poperinghe is built on the latter part of its route over the old Hazebrouck–Poperinghe railway embankment

6

MAJOR LANOE HAWKER V.C. AT ABEELE AERODROME
Watou, West Flanders, Belgium.

ABEELE IS A TYPICAL FLEMISH VILLAGE differing from most in that it once embraced the customs-post that monitored the Belgian side of the frontier-crossing with France. During the Great War, it sat on one of the main British supply routes to the Western Front due in the main to its proximity to Poperinghe and the front-line further east around Ypres. Convoys of men, artillery, horses and supplies of all types would surge through the narrow streets *en route* towards the front. Everything needed to meet the needs of a modern army which, increasing in size weekly, used Abeele as part of its principal avenue of supply.

Usually safe from enemy bombardment, Abeele escaped the ravages of shelling which was the sad reward of so many of the small communities in the immediate war zone. Out of range of the largest calibre enemy artillery, it enjoyed a fairly normal and undisturbed daily existence, if the perpetual rumblings of massive military convoys passing by could be described as 'normal and undisturbed'. However, enemy aircraft frequently visited under cover of darkness, searching out the military camps and supply dumps they knew to be sited around the railway complex at Remi Sidings, Lijssenthoek situated slightly to the north.

Sited south-west of the village just off the main Poperinghe-Steenvoorde road, the local aerodrome and its operational Royal Flying Corps squadron was a priority target, with its many supply and support units essential for servicing the squadrons stationed in and around the airfield.

A military convoy making its way through Abeele high street during the war

Number 6 Squadron, Royal Flying Corps operated from the aerodrome during 1915-16. Its duties were: one, acting as observation for the ground forces; two, keeping the skies clear of enemy planes over the back areas; and three, flying sorties over the trench-lines around the Ypres Salient. While serving with the squadron, Major Lanoe George Hawker took air-warfare into a new dimension by attaching a Lewis machine-gun to the side of his airplane. It was a "first" in airplane armament development.

Lanoe George Hawker, son of Lieutenant Henry Colley Hawker, Royal Navy, was born at Longparish, Hampshire on 30th December 1890. In July 1905, he followed in his father's footsteps by taking up military education at the Royal Naval College, Dartmouth. Later, due to ill health, he was forced to discontinue his studies, a great disappointment to his father and himself. Early in 1910 he again took up his education but this time at the Royal Military College, Woolwich, from where in July 1911 he was commissioned into the Royal Engineers. As early as 1910 he had joined the Royal Aero Club but, due to the demands of his engineering studies, he only passed his pilot's test in March 1913. At the beginning of August 1914, he followed his new-found love of flying and transferred from the Royal Engineers to the Royal Flying Corps, moving to the Central Flying School at Upavon near Salisbury Plain where he became a Flight Commander.

Early 1915 found him based at the Abeele airfield where he was promoted to Squadron Commander. He took to the new service as to the manner born doing sterling work over St. Julien spotting for the artillery in the Second Battle of Ypres. He was awarded the Distinguished Service Order in April 1915 for flying a lone bombing mission over German airship sheds at Gontrode near Ghent in enemy occupied Flanders. With the arrival of the improved version of the Bristol Scout at Abeele in 1916, he noted in his diary: "I have a beautiful little toy, a new Bristol Scout aeroplane that goes at 80 m.p.h. and climbs at 5/6000ft. per minute. I will have a M.G. fitted and see how the Hun likes that".

He did exactly that. These were the early days of air warfare with opposing flyers firing darts or infantry rifles at each other and

Aerial view of Abeele Aerodrome in 1915 when 6 Squadron R.F.C. were in residence

dropping light bombs through openings in the fuselage, but always maintaining a high level of chivalry. Hawker, by fixing a Lewis gun to the side of his plane, soon cast aside this somewhat cavalier attitude. As the gun was fitted to pan away from the propellers it prompted him into developing a method of attack with a side-on approach. Although many German aeroplanes were fitted with machine-guns it can be safely said that his concept was part-cause for taking the airplane into a new dimension from which it would rapidly progress to what is today the most important arm in military conflict.

The Lewis gun gave him an edge, and in July of 1915, he attacked three enemy aircraft single-handed over the Menin Road, driving-off one and downing the other two, winning the Victoria Cross, one of the first won by the new service.[1]

For all his prowess as an aggressor he was not insensitive to the fate he caused the enemy flyers he shot down. On 1st August 1915, in a letter to his brother Tyrell then serving with the artillery up in the Ypres Salient, he said "I felt very sorry for him when he fell in flames, but war is war, and they (the Germans) have been very troublesome of late."

His initiative had contributed much to the progress and development of methods of strategic and tactical flying. He initiated low-flash spotting for the artillery and in-depth solo reconnaissance; he invented a ring-sight for the guns which automatically allowed for deflection; he caused the Lewis gun ammunition drum to be modified and doubled its content. He even helped design the fleece-lined flying boots which were to become standard issue for military pilots. He was predominant in creating and developing the 'down-sun' attack which would be honed and added to by all the great flying aces who would follow after his death in 1916. Major "Mick" Mannock, Britain's top 'Ace', with 73 kills to his credit, always used the 'down-sun' approach and made it a cardinal rule to teach his pupils the same.

Major Hawker was one of the earlier flying aces and after shooting down seven enemy aircraft in the Ypres sector he was transferred to northern France in the Somme sector taking command of 24 Squadron, Royal Flying Corps at Bertangles near Amiens, then being kept busy observing for the battling troops at Bapaume. In November 1916, while leading his squadron, he fell before the blazing guns of a rising star of the German Air Force, one Baron Manfred Von Richthofen, the famed Red Baron. Their air duel was one of the most famous of the war, lasting over an hour with Major Hawker holding to his task of defending a group of slow-moving observation planes over Guedecourt near Bapaume. He became the 11th victim of the Red Baron, crashing at Lieusenhof Farm on the road to Flers and was buried there by German gunners. He was first reported as missing and afterwards, confirmed on 27th July 1917, as killed in November 1916. His grave was lost in the shelling of later battles and his name is commemorated on the Arras Memorial to the Missing at Fauborge D'Amiens Cemetery.[2]

The Abeele Aerodrome that he left behind was never as active a base as its neighbour at Proven, north-east of Poperinghe. It would appear to have had an imperfect landing strip and now the uneven surface is used for cattle-grazing. It is difficult to imagine today those young pilots fresh out of training, attempting to land on this area. The visitor with the more fertile mind should be forgiven if the Flanders winds sweeping across the flatlands through the lines of trees acting as windbreaks, bring to mind the hustle, bustle and noises of those days long gone.

Royal Flying Corps pilots knew a different war from that of the soldier. It was experienced in short bursts in the air, alone in a cockpit, then would come a return to comfortable quarters, and tempered with the joy of flying, an activity only the favoured few experienced in those years. But theirs could be a lonely, violent death, often without the solace of a decent burial and, if they were to be buried, it was often by the enemy, having fallen over his territory. For the many of them who avoided death, but who became casualties, theirs was a destiny to suffer wounds of the most ghastly nature, both physical and psychological.

Some of the farm buildings close to the old airstrip were used as mess facilities and billets for the crews, mechanics, supporting units and other squadron personnel. Except for these, little is left to convey the noise, movement and intense activity that created the ambience of a small airfield like Abeele in the war years. It is doubtful whether Abeele, or its cemetery, are high on the list of places pilgrims to the Western Front wish to visit. No great actions were fought here and the name Abeele only appears in regimental histories and books as a place for passing through or marching past. Nevertheless, if travelling via Steenvoorde on a visit to Ypres, it is worthwhile making the detour to the cemetery to take time to stand and reflect. In 1915, air warfare was in its infancy, few military commanders took it seriously and the troops on the ground didn't appreciate what they were witnessing as the tiny spots, Allied and enemy alike, buzzed around in the sky eventually breaking-off to make their way back to their airfields, places such as the airstrip at Abeele. It was at places like this that the forerunners of today's jet fighters were serviced, repaired or broken. It was here that the pilots met together to discuss what could be achieved with their flying machines, and it was here that they celebrated their successes or grieved for those who did not return - but it was in the air that they learned how to fight and survive. Many of the pilots, both Allied and enemy, used well their experiences of the Great War to influence their respective air force performances in the war that followed twenty odd years later.

Just south of the old aerodrome is Abeele Aerodrome Military Cemetery. Small by Western Front standards, it wasn't used by the Royal Flying Corps, although it would be natural to presume that some fatalities would have found a resting place in a nearby plot. Then again, Abeele's position close to the casualty clearing stations at Godewaersvelde in France and Remi Sidings, Lijssenthoek in Belgium, suggested there were enough facilities to cope with whatever demands were made by a local aerodrome.

The cemetery was begun in 1918 and used by both the French and the British when it was expected that the German advances south of Ypres during the Battle of the Lys might threaten the British back area.[3] After the Armistice the French removed their dead from Abeele to their Potijze cemetery and the Americans moved theirs to the Flanders Fields Cemetery at Wareghem.

The American army used the cemetery in 1918. 84 men of the 104th machine-gun Company, 27th (New York) Division were buried there after their action on the Vierstraat Ridge in August 1918.[4] They rested in the cemetery until the early 1920s when they were moved to Wareghem. A feature of the cemetery is the clear lawn at its far end. Originally Plot III, it housed the graves of those Americans and, on their departure, it was never re-used.

Notes :

1. His Gazette of 24th August, 1915 read:

Lanoe George Hawker, Capt., R.E. and R.F.C. Date of Act of Bravery; 25th July, 1915. For most conspicuous bravery and very great ability on the 25th July 1915. When flying alone he attacked three German aeroplanes in succession. The first managed eventually to escape, the second was driven to the ground damaged, and the third, which he attacked at a height of about 10,000 feet, was driven to earth in our lines, the pilot and observer being killed. The personal bravery shown by this officer was of the very highest order, as the enemy's aircraft were armed with machine-guns, and all carried a passenger as well as the pilot.

2. Also commemorated on the Arras Memorial to the Missing at Fauberge D'Amiens Cemetery is Major Edward "Mick" Mannock V.C. Mannock the new C.O. of 85 Squadron (St. Omer) was hit by ground fire at dawn over Bois Pacaut when downing his final victim. His grave was lost in later shelling. He was awarded a V.C. in 1919 after lobbying by his former comrades and a passionate plea in the House of Commons by Winston Churchill. The grave of the Unknown Aviator at Laventie is thought possibly to be that of the Major Mannock.

3, In April and May, 1918 the French buried 99of their troops and four British officers in Plot I, but they removed dead after the Armistice. Plot I now contains the four British officers and 25 British soldiers who were originally buried in April-August 1918 in a French extension of Boeschêpe Churchyard. Plot II contains 75 British graves of troops buried in July - August 1918. Plot III originally contained the graves of 84 American soldiers who fell at Vierstraat in 1918, and who were removed to the American Flanders Fields Cemetery in Wareghem.

4. In 1956, an American veteran of the 104th machine-gun Company, 27th (New York) Division visited the cemetery while on a pilgrimage with his wife. He was upset to find that his comrades-in-arms buried after the Vierstraat action were not there. He became very emotional when, due to language difficulties with the locals he could not determine what had happened to them. It was only after exhaustive enquiries that he was able to trace them to the Flanders Fields cemetery where he was at last able to pay his respects to his long lost friends.

Abeele Aerodrome Military Cemetery showing the empty Plot III where were buried American troops of the 104th machine-gun Company, 27th (New York) Division

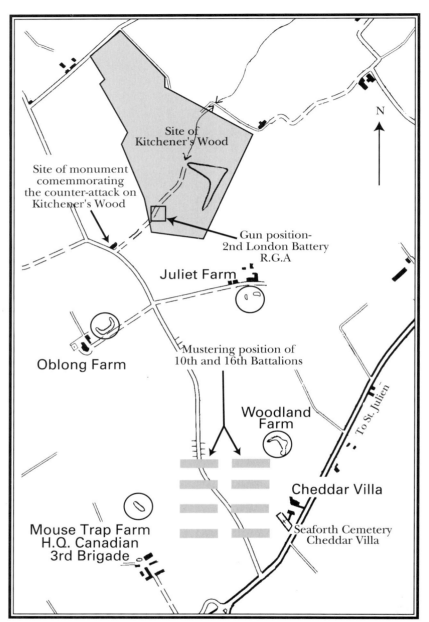

The points encircled on this map of the area as it is today identify the remnants of the original farm complex positions as they were during the war. See map on page 62 for the original configuration.

7
16th BATTALION (THE CANADIAN SCOTTISH)
AT KITCHENER'S WOOD
St.Julien, 22nd April 1915

THE 3RD CANADIAN INFANTRY BRIGADE had been at Estaires from 1st to 5th April 1915 under training in front-line trench acclimatisation before moving to billets around Cassel. On the morning of 10th April, 1915, General Sir Horace Smith-Dorrien, Commander Second Army, inspected the brigade in the hill-top town, informing the battalions that they were to relieve the French XI Division holding a line in the Poelcappelle sector of the Ypres Salient. On 12th April, they received orders to move into the Salient to conduct the relief.

One of the brigade's battalions, the kilted 16th (The Canadian Scottish), was formed from the pre-war reserves of four company size militia units from Victoria, Vancouver, Winnipeg and Ontario. By chance, these four units were Scottish - the 50th Gordons, 72nd Seaforths, 79th Cameron and 91st Argyll and Sutherland Highlanders and were soon dubbed The Canadian Scottish, a name borne proudly, and officially, in their title ever since.[1]

On the evening of 14th April, an advance party left Cassel to set-up the battalion's part of the relief, followed by the rest of the men who marched to Steenvoorde on the afternoon of the 15th. Here they stayed overnight before embussing to Vlamertinghe, from where they marched to Wieltje. Later that evening they moved through St. Julien to take over their sector of trenches right-of-the-line north of the town. On the 17th they set about improving their new position. In the meantime, 3rd Brigade command had set up headquarters in a farm, map reference

C.22.b, just north of Wieltje. Farm C.22.b was later to gain fame under the name Mouse Trap Farm.[2]

On the 20th, the battalion was relieved and placed in divisional reserve in Ypres and La Brique, a small hamlet just north of the town, east of the Yser Canal. During the relief, a Captain Rae reported to battalion headquarters that the profile of the German parapet had changed and now had openings along its line.[3] The report was noted but nobody knew of a reason for the change.

In the afternoon of the 22nd, the front north and west of St. Julien, and Ypres itself, came under heavy shelling. Then all roads leading northward from the town came under shrapnel fire. At 5.30 p.m., 3rd Brigade Headquarters ordered the 16th Battalion to 'Stand To Arms', and to move to positions, out of the danger area.

Shortly, troops of the French Algerian infantry, bareheaded, and with no weapons or equipment, came streaming over the canal followed by French and Belgian artillery with empty limbers, the drivers coughing and spluttering. Crowds of civilians were rushing among the horses, and the local inhabitants, after speaking to

Farm C.22.b, Mouse Trap Farm today, rebuilt after the war approximately 200 yards south of its original site which still contains part of its surrounding moat. Oblong Farm is in the far right background with the white panel in its roof.

them, gathered what possessions they could and followed them. Men of the battalion tried to get information from the French who, pointing to their throats, offered nothing but coughing and gasping, their eyes streaming and showing signs of abject terror. Lieutenant-Colonel Leckie, the battalion commander, realising that something desperate had happened, prepared for action, issuing extra ammunition and emergency rations. He then deployed the battalion along the western bank of the canal in preparation for he knew not what.

Unknown to them, the line held by the French 87th Territorial and the 45th Algerian Divisions had disintegrated before a chlorine gas attack, a floating cloud of death, followed by an infantry onslaught which had penetrated the British line to a depth of two-and-a-half miles, the extreme left of the line having fallen back to a point close to Steenstraat south-west of Bixschoote.

Pilckem and Langemarck had fallen, Keerselare, St. Julien and Wieltje were under threat, with St. Jean next in line and then – Ypres. The way was open for the victory the German armies had been chasing since 1914 – but the 1st Canadian Division had other plans, even though its left flank, held by their 3rd Brigade, and once adjoined to the right flank of the fleeing Algerian Division, was now wide open with the Germans moving into its rear.

About 7.40 p.m., the 16th was ordered to get to 3rd Brigade Headquarters at Farm C.22.b, as fast as possible.

By 8 p.m., it was on the move and, unknowingly, was hurrying forward to carve out for itself a unique place in military history.

The quickest route lay through St. Jean, but heavy shelling caused a detour through La Brique - the Canadians being totally unaware of the fact that they, and a few other units, were the only British troops between the enemy and Ypres on a front of 7,000 yards.[4] Traffic blocking Wieltje added to the delay in reaching headquarters but, around 10 p.m., the battalion arrived and mustered in a field close by, still unaware of what was in store for it. The men felt a tightening and dryness of the throat and their eyes began to smart and water. Nobody had any idea as to the reason for this and just accepted it as part of their lot.

Lieutenant-Colonel Leckie reported to the Brigade Commander and was ordered to form up his battalion 30 yards behind the 10th Battalion, who had arrived at the headquarters shortly after 9 p.m. and were in formation, ready for action to support an attack by the French 46th Division. In the event, the French attack did not materialise leaving the Canadians completely isolated.

The objective was to capture an enemy trench south of a wood to their north at map reference C.10.d., called Bois des Cuisiniers (later Kitchener's Wood, a not very accurate translation of its French name) due west of St. Julien. This done, both units were to continue the attack and take the wood, bearing left once in it to clear the enemy from the section that branched out to the north-west. The wood appeared as a faint, shadowy mass on the moonlit but darkening skyline. Their direction, given in simplistic terms by Brigade-Major L. C. G. B. Hughes, was to "follow the North Star".

The men of both battalions in an attacking formation much practised by the 16th during their training spell at Estaires, but not necessarily the right one for such an attack as was about to be launched, were ordered to fix bayonets, an order which gave them some idea as to what to expect in the near future.

Two battalions in eight waves were to attack (following the North Star) across open ground, the condition of which they could not see, in an untested formation, against a trench-line and an occupied wood of which they had no intelligence, with no idea of the strength of the enemy they were facing, in support of a French attack which didn't take place, the only factor in their favour being that the enemy did not know they were coming – with the success of the attack depending totally on its element of surprise.

This apparent lack of planning was caused by the desperate situation facing the Canadian 1st Division following the gas attack. Time was of the essence and the enemy occupying Kitchener's Wood, the only area of cover in its position on the ridge of high ground called Mauser Ridge, was considered unacceptable, hence the urgency, and seeming lack of planning, of the attack decision. At 11.45 p.m. the attack, supported by what little artillery was available, was launched.

The battalions had to cover 800 to 1,000 yards of ground, and this, they were to discover, was cross-hatched with ditches and hedgerows, lit only by the stars and a setting moon. Stumbling over ditches, breaking formation to pass through openings in hedges, reforming and moving on, the attack force made good progress, apparently unnoticed by the enemy ahead of them.

About 200 yards from the objective they encountered a wire-threaded hedge and the noise made in breaking through this alerted the enemy who, in the light of the flares they released, first saw this mass of determined troops, with bayonets fixed, rushing at them. The Canadians, now completely exposed in the brittle light of the enemy flares, took both rifle and machine-gun fire, cutting down their first waves with men falling left and right, the bullet-ridden bodies impeding the rush of those following. The ranks wavered for an instant, with companies of both battalions becoming mixed with each other, but they didn't stop. They surged forward, ripped into and across the German trenches and cheering, shouting and yelling they lunged into the wood using bayonet, rifle-butt and bomb with devastating effect. Individual, close-combat fighting spread throughout the shattered, bullet-scarred oak tree woodland with the Canadians decimating two German infantry battalions with the ferocity of their attack, and silencing a good number of machine-gun nests in the doing.

The order to bear left in the wood went by the board. The 10th went straight through it and into a field on its northern edge, clearing everything in its path. The 16th forged ahead and to the right, intent on clearing a trench on the right-front of the wood which was laying down fire on them. When they were within 30 or 40 yards of this trench, the occupiers, very sensibly, ceased firing and fled, the sight of the screaming, yelling, kilted Canadians with fixed bayonets prompting their decision.

Confusion reigned within the wood, with parties of men working their way through it, indulging in savage hand-to-hand fighting, attacking anyone and anything that wasn't Canadian, one party actually charging the dark shapes of four British guns of the 2nd London Battery R.G.A. left abandoned with the coming of the gas, but it was soon all over. The Canadians had taken a fortified position and had cleared it of crack troops of the 2nd Prussian Guard and the battle-seasoned men of the 234th Bavarian Infantry Regiment. Nevertheless, they had suffered staggering casualties and the approaches to the wood were littered with their dead.

Even though the victors, they found themselves in a serious situation. The French attack they were supposed to support hadn't happened, and now the lack of attack planning took its toll. Both battalions had lost up to 50% of their strength in the charge, and every company commander had been hit. The resulting thinness in command, with units mixing with each other in the darkness, made it difficult to consolidate. The Canadians now found themselves occupying a large wood with not enough men to hold it, a great deal of wounded to tend to, both of their flanks exposed, and heavy fire raking them from all sides. The north-west section of the wood had not been completely cleared and the enemy, in strength, held a trench running westward from the south-west corner, with a redoubt about 15 yards from the left of the trench they had cleared in front of the wood.

The men were difficult to control, flushed with victory and looking for a fight, they were making sorties, individually and in groups, and some were just searching for friends and comrades to have a chat about recent events. The remaining officers decided to withdraw from the wood and set-up a defence line in the 200 yards of trench on its southern edge, leaving posts in the wood to guard the guns. This withdrawal was completed by 4 a.m. on the 23rd and reinforcements were called for, including a request for men and horses to retrieve the British guns. This request went unfulfilled and later in the night patrols covered a party of engineers who destroyed the guns. The patrols stayed in the wood to maintain contact with the enemy should he return.

The 10th battalion took over the left of the trench while the 16th took the right, extending it to the north-east by men lying in the field and digging themselves gun-pits. A second line of defence was set-up 150 yards further back and battalion headquarters, plus a first aid post, were set up in the ruins of a farm (Oblong Farm). The two battalions, with a combined tally of only 451 men, were now ready to face anything that was to come.

Attempts were made to make contact to their right, where the left of the Canadian 1st Division line should have been, but the enemy were found to be there instead - and in strength. German flares were lighting the areas to their left and rear, so, to all intents and purposes, they were surrounded.

It was decided that they would stay put, hold the line and hope for the reinforcements. Somewhere between 2.30 and 3 a.m., the 2nd Battalion under Lieutenant-Colonel Watson arrived and reinforced the right of the line, with one company making an attempt to capture the German positions at the south-west corner of the wood. This proved unsuccessful, as were attempts by Lieutenant Tupper, the 16th Battalion's machine-gun officer to bring enfilade fire to bear. Tupper's party found itself practically surrounded, and under fire. One of his gun team had his hand smashed, and later found fourteen bullet-holes in his kilt. During the night, Lieutenant Tupper was hit and had to drag himself back to the Canadian lines. The enemy captured the machine-gun but not before it was rendered useless by the gun team.

During the early part of the night there was much activity. Stretcher bearers, ration parties and orderlies were moving up and this contact with their reinforcements gave the troops a certain sense of security, but their tactical position had not improved. Men were consolidating the trench and adjusting themselves to the situation. The dead were lifted over the parapet and the wounded made as comfortable as possible under the prevailing conditions. Sections of both battalions moved back, under cover of a patch of mustard, to the second line near Battalion Headquarters and the First Aid Post at Oblong Farm.

At 5.30 a.m., an enemy aircraft spotted the movement and called in his artillery fire. The results were disastrous, with men being blown up in all directions and the crowded headquarters and First Aid Post being turned into a complete shambles.

With the coming of daylight on the 23rd, the night's appalling harvest had been revealed to the men holding their new lines of

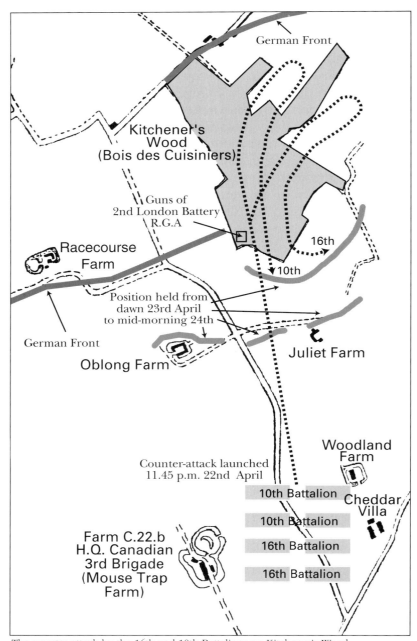

The counter-attack by the 16th and 10th Battalions on Kitchener's Wood

defence. Row upon row of uniformed dead were lying behind the trench - men of 16th Battalion identified by the tartan of the kilt, the yellow stripe of the Gordons, the white of the Seaforths, the red of the Camerons, and the dark green of the Argylls, with the khaki-clad bodies of the 10th Battalion mingled amongst them.

All in all, an ominous start to the day, but nothing untoward was to happen even though the German position to the south-west of the wood presented an ominous threat. Men of the 2nd, 16th and 10th Battalions, with new reinforcements from the 3rd battalion worked all day at consolidating the line until the late evening when the enemy opened a period of rapid fire, but with no following attack. For some reason he chose not to exploit the opportunity made with his gas-driven breakthrough. Daylight closed for the Canadians with the line in front of the wood strengthened, but still with open flanks.

Dawn of the 24th saw the German change of mind – the whole Canadian line from St. Julien to Gravenstafel came under massive gas, artillery and infantry attacks as they strove to eliminate the Canadian position and the Ypres Slient. All this was to no avail, the Canadians held and by mid-morning the sorely depleted ranks of the 16th and 10th Battalions withdrew to re-organise, the 16th to trenches west of Farm C.22.b and the 10th to those near 2nd Brigade Headquarters at Pond Farm. This withdrawal wasn't allowed to pass without the Germans heralding the event with incessant machine-gun fire and frenzied activity from their well-positioned snipers. Nevertheless the men of the 10th and 16th made it back across the open ground, so ending their involvement with Kitchener's Wood.

Much was to be done before the danger of a breakthrough would be eliminated. Many costly, ill-prepared, poorly-supported counter-attacks were conducted along the Mauser Ridge west of where the 16th and 10th had clung to their captured trench in front of Kitchener's Wood. British and Canadian troops were slaughtered in these heroic attacks along the broken line but, in the end, it was re-formed although well behind its original position. The quick-thinking and fast decision-making of the

Canadian Command, although having a seemingly 'flying by the seat of the pants' feel about it, was essential under the critical circumstances of the time. This, combined with the fortitude, tenacity and the pure fighting ability of the Canadian battalions, as shown by the 16th and 10th at Kitchener's Wood, were the factors that filled the gap in the line – chlorine gas or not – once more denying the Kaiser's move to the Channel ports.

Of the 16th and 10th Battalions, General Ferdinand Foch, Allied Supreme Commander, spoke for all when he said he considered the attack on Kitchener's Wood as "the finest act in the war."

Notes:

1. Today's Militia unit, the Canadian Scottish Regiment (Princess Mary's) is deeply proud of its origins from these four units and, coupled with the Calgary Highlanders (the 10th Battalion of the Great War), is entitled to wear on its uniform the Oak Leaf and Acorn – the Battle Honour commemorating the action at Kitchener's Wood.

The cap badge of the 16th Battalion (The Canadian Scottish) worn as collar dogs by today's Canadian Scottish Regiment. The regiment's modern cap badge features 16 maple leaves to perpetuate the memory of the 16th Battalion.

2. Map reference C.22.b, known to the Belgians and French as Château du Nord, to the Germans as Wieltje Farm and to the British as Shell Trap Farm (some British units called it Canadian Farm). Shell Trap Farm was considered an ill-omen so it was changed by V Corps to Mouse Trap Farm.

Practically all the farm names appearing on British Trench Maps were designated during and after the April-May 1915 battles and were not featured on maps at the time. Mouse Trap Farm was never known as such during the Second Battle of Ypres, it was simply called Farm C.22.b.

3. The 13th and 15th Canadian Battalions on the morning of April 22nd reported to 43rd Brigade Headquarters that pipes were projecting through the German parapet. This information was passed on to Divisional Headquarters, but no idea was formed of their purpose.

4. The 16th Battalion, a few companies of the Middlesex Regiment, three companies of the 14th Canadian Battalion, the 3rd Field Company Canadian Engineers, the 3rd Canadian Infantry Brigade Bombing Company, and 3rd Canadian Infantry Brigade Headquarters was the total complement of British forces available to face the enemy should he attack on the 7,000 yard front.

The memorial to the 10th and 16th Battalion's counter-attack at Kitchener's Wood. Ignace and Francine Bentien-Heyman kindly donated the land on which it stands, just where the south-west tip of where Kitchener's Wood was sited, and just to the left of their home at Wijngaardstraat 2, Langemarck, Sint. Juliaan (St. Julien). It was unveiled on 22nd March 1997, a month short of eighty-two years after the day the Germans created havoc in the British front line with their use of chlorine gas as a weapon - and the same period of time after the night that, for the Canadian forces, the 10th and 16th Battalions began the long and bitter struggle to fill the gap it caused.

65

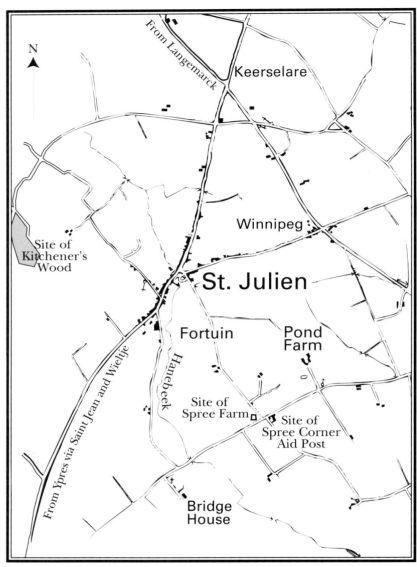

In April 1915, during the Second Battle of Ypres, the Canadian 1st Division held the line after filling the gap caused by the German poison gas attack. Brigadier General Arthur Currie, commanding the 2nd Infantry Brigade, used Pond Farm as his head-quarters during this critical period. Although not fortified during the Second Battle of Ypres, the Germans had turned it into a veritable fortress in the years following. During the Third Battle of Ypres, it was a major obstacle to the British advance and was only captured on 20th September 1917

8

POND FARM
Fortuin, St. Julien, Ypres, 1915-1917

IN ANY DETAILED STUDY OF THE BATTLES which raged around Ypres during the Great War it is evident how important were the locations of the many farms and rural holdings in the meadows around the town. The Germans, in residence since the early stages of the war, had organised their defences in these farmsteads. They made full use of the deep cellars normally found under the main farm buildings and supplemented them later in the war by designing a comprehensive chain of concrete bunkers, shelters and pill-boxes around them, converting each complex of farm buildings into a self-contained mini-fortress. The tactical siting of these strongpoints, utilising those farms on a rise in the ground, on the banks of one of the many streams which crossed the area, or those in flat areas with a good field of fire, were intended to present serious obstacles for the Allied command if it attempted to break the grip that the Germans had on the environs of the old town of Ypres - yet unless the attempt to do so was made the war would stagger into a muddy stalemate.

One such strongpoint, just south-east of the village of St Julien, was called Pond Farm. This farm gained prominence for itself during the Second Battle of Ypres in 1915 and the bruising Passchendaele campaign of 1917.

Today, a prosperous farm property on the left hand side of the secondary road leading to the hamlet of Gravenstafel from the village of Wieltje, it has but one feature as a reminder of its former status - a concrete shelter situated just within the farm entrance.[1]

A small shrine sits at the entrance to the farm's driveway and further along the drive in the field to the left is a pond. British army cartographers were not slow to appropriate this feature to establish the name Pond Farm as another military map reference.

In April of 1915, activities around Pond Farm were hectic. During the Second Battle of Ypres the Germans, using poison gas, had broken the Allied line along the Pilckem Ridge, sending columns of French Colonial troops fleeing to the rear in disarray. The Canadian 1st Division were to win undying fame by filling the vital gap in the British line thus helping to save Ypres itself. Their new line, making up their left flank, was formed west of Pond Farm running south of, and across the western side of Kitchener's Wood, then north of Vancouver Crossroads and Keerselare, covering the St. Julien-Poelcappelle road. The Commander of the Canadian 2nd Infantry Brigade, destined to become Sir Arthur Currie Commander of the Canadian Corps at the war's end, was a Brigadier-General at this period. Pond Farm was the headquarters of the 2nd Infantry Brigade at the opening of the gas attack and, at a vital stage in the proceedings, Brigadier-General Currie organised and conducted the defence of the locality from the farm. The weeks following the opening of the attack was a desperate period of crushing and confusing attack and counter-attack. Reserves were rushed in from other British sectors in a bid to stem the enemy advance and to fight one of the great delaying actions of 1915.

On 25th April, units of the British 11th Brigade, 4th Division were called in from the Ploegsteert area to relieve the Canadians, amongst them the 1st Battalions of the Rifle Brigade and the London Rifle Brigade. The former were professionals, bloodied at Mons and Le Cateau and tempered in the retreat to the River Marne the summer before, whereas their territorial compatriots of the London Rifle Brigade had only arrived in Belgium just before Christmas 1914.

The roads they took to the Pond Farm area, as well as having suffered from continual shell-fire for many days, were choked with ambulances and walking wounded. Confusion and congestion reigned. At St. Jean, weary Canadians filtering back through the incoming riflemen heard a Rifle Brigade machine-gunner shouting to another of his section: "Are we downhearted?". "No" the other yelled. A Canadian, a great deal wiser after recent experience in the line, called out: "You damn soon will be".

At Spree Farm crossroads, just before Pond Farm, the Rifle Brigade was led by Canadian guides to positions on Hill 37 south-east of the farm. Meanwhile, men of London Rifle Brigade, acting in a supporting roll, took up their positions closer to Pond Farm itself.

The Rifle Brigade passed the night quietly enough but in the early dawn an enemy bombardment began and lasted intermittently until the 28th when the battalion were moved forward to the northern slopes of Hill 37 and dug trenches running north-east to the Hanebeek river. The following three days were fairly quiet, but the battalion was under threat of attack the whole time and, during the late afternoon on 2nd May they were subjected to a bombardment at almost point-blank range from the Gravenstafel Ridge only 1,000 yards away.

Communications with brigade headquarters were broken down and trenches were demolished, with those either side of the Hanebeek left in a desperate condition. Every man in the northern section of the trench was wounded and only four in the southern part were capable of firing a rifle. Other regiments of the 11th Brigade extended the hastily-erected defensive-line in the sector and in this fashion and, under tremendous pressure, the enemy advance was halted. Finally, at dusk on 3rd May, orders were received to withdraw. During the withdrawal, a wounded Captain Railston, helped by Sergeant Ford and Acting-Corporal Ellingham, kept off the Germans by running up and down the trench firing rifles all along it. For this, Captain Railston was subsequently awarded the D.S.O. and Ford and Ellingham each the D.C.M.

Meanwhile, the London Rifle Brigade battalion who had taken up positions early on the morning of 26th April south of the Wieltje-Fortuin road just below Pond Farm experienced heavy shelling from both the north and east. At dusk they moved to a new line filling a gap between a detachment of about 250 men from about six different units. They stayed in these trenches throughout the 27th when orders were received to assist the Rifle Brigade and to occupy part of the trench lines on Hill 37. The 1st of May was spent readjusting and consolidating trench lines, caring for the wounded and burying the dead. They came under more shelling on the 2nd and later in the day were subjected to a gas attack followed by an infantry attack. By now, the battalion was exhausted, not having slept for seven nights. The next day they took intermittent shelling before orders were received to evacuate their positions. At 12.45 a.m. on the morning of 4th May, the battalion moved out of the line, the last troops of the 11th Brigade troops to do so.

The enemy paid dearly for advantages gained at Hill 37, Pond Farm and the Gravenstafel ridge - but so did the two British rifle battalions. Losses were recorded as: 1st Battalion Rifle Brigade, 400 officers and other ranks and the 1st Battalion London Rifle Brigade, 408 officers and other ranks. An unsung hero who made his way back was Captain G. E. Ferguson R.A.M.C., Medical Officer to the 1st Battalion Rifle Brigade. It was said of him, "He was truly magnificent, Victoria Crosses have been won for less than he did". The Battalion report added:

> His battalion aid post was at the notorious Spree Farm Cross Roads (Fortuin). Not only did the M.O. establish and maintain his aid post for all cases passing through over several traumatic days, but organised a separate advanced aid post for severely wounded, where in addition to medical attention they were supplied with hot drinks and food [2]

Most of the ground fought over during this action from the 22nd April to the 4th May was given-up following the withdrawal of the British force and the new Allied line left Pond Farm in the hands of the Germans.

Actions in July to September 1917 would again see the farm, now a German strongpoint sporting a surround of dugouts complemented by a concrete bunker in its forecourt, flare into prominence as once more the farm area would consume British lives. It would be the enemy who this time who would generally control proceedings. Men from the 55th (West Lancashire) Division, notably the 8th Battalion King's Liverpool (Irish) Regiment, took heavy losses from the machine-gunners manning the squat and sturdy bunker now protecting the approaches to the Pond Farm area. The 36th (Ulster) Division experienced the same difficulties when relieving the 55th (West Lancashire) Division as the devastated terrain lent itself to efficient defence with one of its battalions, the 14th Battalion Royal Irish Rifles. taking heavy casualties from the guns safely ensconced within the farm complex.

The 2/5th Lancashire Fusiliers, a sister-battalion to the 8th Battalion King's Liverpool (Irish), experienced a particularly torrid time at Pond Farm, losing 500 men from a force of 593. Their commanding officer, Lieutenant-Colonel B. Best-Dunkley was awarded the Victoria Cross for his leadership in the fighting around the farm.

In August, the 184th Brigade, 61st Division had to pass Pond Farm when mounting an attack towards the strongpoints Martha House and Hindu Cottage. The machine-gunners posted at Pond Farm took a devastating toll of their numbers, the 2/4th Berks of that brigade incurred 222 casualties in one hour, including 86 killed and missing.

Many other units were to try to subdue the Pond Farm garrison including, once again, the 8th King's Liverpool (Irish) who had a second attempt repulsed during the September fighting which finally brought about the unlocking of the German defensive system locally.

When the farm finally fell, and was relegated to a backwater in the British rear, it was estimated that, during the period 31st July to 26th September 1917, its infamous defences had accounted for several hundred British lives from various units. It was never fought over again, and Pond Farm, once feared and respected, became just a reference in regimental unit histories.

The concrete-shelter with its protective earth banking on top can be seen at the farm's entrance. This earth-covering was a protective measure used by both Germans and British to act as camouflage and to dilute the effect of shell-fire on the structure. The bunker, usually flooded during the winter months, is now used by cattle for shelter. An area of disturbed earth among the trees to the right of the farm buildings was supposedly used by the German garrisons as a regimental aid station. Although this cannot be authenticated, the 1/4th Loyal North Lancasters, 55th (West Lancashire) Division, set up an aid station on this site, using the existing facilities, during the Third Battle of Ypres.

Notes:

1. In the 1920s, many farmers dismantled the structures on their land using the concrete for hard core and aggregate. Later, the Belgian government prohibited the practice, and so the Pond Farm bunker survived.

2. The aid post at Spree Farm crossroads was one of the busiest in the sector and several units made use of it. No ambulances could reach this advanced and dangerous spot and the wounded poured in day and night for several days of the operation east of Wieltje. Spree Farm Aid Station was on the corner of the road to St. Julien about 150 metres west of Pond Farm. In July 1917 the 8th King's Liverpool (Irish) saw action at Pond Farm. One of its officers, Captain R. Hodson records: "The Medical Officer of the 10th King's Liverpool (Scottish) very busy here attending the wounded". That officer may have been Captain. N. Chavasse V.C. and Bar who, wounded at Setques Farm, died a few days later and was buried in the British Military Cemetery at Brandhoek. Setques Farm is about 300 metres west of Spree Farm crossroads. Bridge House cemetery, sited close to what were the crossroads, was possibly started from the dead of the Spree Farm Aid Post.

,All that is left of the infamous Pond Farm fortifications. Today, the farmer and his cattle use this pill-box in a way never dreamed of by its builders or the various occupiers in the war years. The pill-box still carries the covering of earth originally intended to act as camouflage and to ease shell-impact.

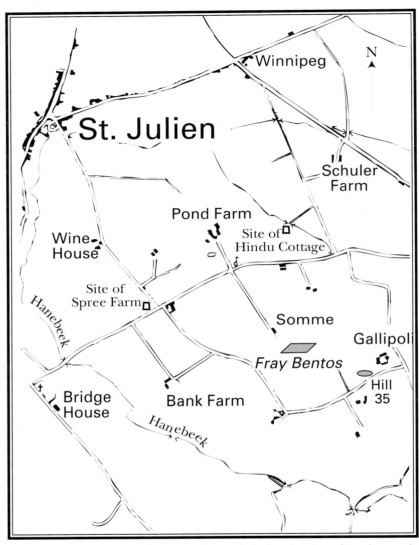

The approximate position where *Fray Bentos* ditched on her line of attack toward Gallipoli. Passing south of Somme Farm she had silenced the garrison of that strongpoint before making her way up the western slope of Hill 35. Had she been successful in overcoming Gallipoli, she would have veered left and eastwards down the hill to Martha House on the lower slopes, south of Kansas Cross. As it was, she remained ditched and fought Gallipoli as a strongpoint in her own right. Her sister tank in the attack, *F.49 (Fairy)*, had made her way back to Starting Point with the wounded of *F.45 (Fiducia)* which she had tried unsuccessfully to tow out of a shell-hole. At Starting Point *F.49 (Fairy)* took a direct hit and was knocked out of the battle.

9
FRAY BENTOS AND GALLIPOLI ON HILL 35
22th August 1917

URING THE THIRD BATTLE OF YPRES, a stunned enemy was under pressure all along the line from Poelcappelle in the north, down through the lower ridges protecting Passchendaele and south across the Menin Road, To their consternation their usual ally, the relentless Flemish rain, for once, did not hold-up the British pressure being applied at all points along the line. It took all the traditional German military ability to resist it. On 19th August, they had been devastated by the destruction of their 'indestructible' group of strongpoints to the north of St. Julien by a British tank and infantry attack.

Even though there was a general resistance by British military commanders to the very concept of tanks, let alone the use of them, the more perceptive among them knew that, after the highly successful attack on the 19th, the method of conducting modern warfare would be changed for all time.

The day after the attack, on 20th August, a section of Mark IV tanks of 'F' Battalion, Tank Corps left their tankodrome at Oesthoek Wood north of Brandhoek on the Ypres–Poperinghe road and travelled as quietly as their Daimler engines would allow, towards the firing-line east of the Ypres Canal, via Bridge 4 near Brielen, then on to Wieltje and St. Jean, to arrive near Spree Corner in the Pond Farm area.

The relatively new machines of war had made good progress in the flickering light of spasmodic shell-fire along the hard road surfaces from the canal. The light rains pattering against the tanks' metal surfaces were in keeping with the sombre thoughts of the ever-watchful and alert crew encased within. What was to unfold at dawn on 22nd August on the battered slopes of nearby Hill 35 would be a drama of grit and determination which will live forever in the annals of the Tank Corps.

The Germans had held on to several important positions at Hill 35 which gave them important observation over the area of Pond Farm, Schuler Farm, Schuler Galleries, the Langemarck road and the approaches to Gravenstafel and Passchendaele, and they were determined to keep control of them. The objectives for the tanks, working with the infantry, would be the wrapping up of this opposition and clearing the enemy from the slopes of this tactically important eminence. Observation from here had allowed the enemy to control the counter-attacks on the 31st July, the opening day of the Third Battle of Ypres, and caused problems for British units along the Steenbeek River near St. Julien. It had almost stopped a vital breakthrough. The view from the crown of the hill was, and still is, most impressive and whoever sat on the crest, as history had demonstrated, had a singular say in local events.

The attack objectives for the tanks, working in pairs, and with infantry support were:

F.42 (FAUN) and *F.46 (FAY)* – Commanded by 2/Lts. R. W. Peters and G. H. Brooks respectively – Pond Farm, Kinder Cottage, Schuler Gallery and Schuler Farm.

F.45 (FIDUCIA) and *F. 47 (FOAM)* – Commanded by 2/Lts. H. Pearson and F. Harris respectively – along Gravenstafel Road to Schuler Gallery.

F.43 (FRITZ PHLATTNER) and *F.48 (FIARA)* – Commanded by 2/Lts. S. C. Harding and G. W. Phillips respectively - Dugouts at 13.b.2.7; 13.d.1.6; Kansas House, Cross Cottages to 13.b.4.6.

F. 41 (FRAY BENTOS) and *F. 49 (FAIRY)* – Commanded by 2/Lts. G. Hill and E. P. Ireland respectively – Somme, Gallipoli, Martha House to 14.c.4.9

At 4.45 a.m. on 22nd August, the tanks set-off from the Starting Point just in front of Capricorn Trench in rear of Spree Farm, The 'F' Battalion Section Commander, Captain Richardson, had opted to go along as a passenger to ascertain the progress and ability of his protégé Lieutenant Hill as commander of *F.41, Fray Bentos*. Crossing the start line, the tanks spread out to mount their attacks on their objectives, and *Fray Bentos* began to ascend Hill 35 just south of its first target, the Somme Farm strongpoint. The hill was soon to become a ferment of fire as the gun-fights broke out between the various strongpoints and the tanks. Somme Farm had held-out against many infantry attacks, its machine-guns keeping the area before it free of invaders, but the tanks fanning-out in full view, together with a fierce little gun-fight, convinced the garrison that their latest visitors were definitely not to be welcomed. As *Fray Bentos* opened fire with its left 6-pounder, they quickly vacated their strongpoint, running back to the safety of their main-lines near the Langemarck–Zonnebeke road. The defenders of Gallipoli on the crest were made of sterner stuff and, seeing that the final defence of Hill 35 would fall on their shoulders they decided to make a fight of it.

The heavy fire from the Gallipoli garrison's large calibre machine-guns smacked against the pitted hull of *Fray Bentos*. The crew in the oppressive, crowded interior were forced to search for cover as best they could as sparks and slivers of metal flew all about them, making for a very unhealthy environment. Armour-piercing bullets were making life very uncomfortable inside *Fray Bentos* and one, piercing the tank's sides, seriously wounded Lieutenant Hill in the neck. Captain Richardson, in attempting to assist his junior colleague, clambered over him to take over the tank's steering mechanism but fouled the controls and the tank ditched. For a moment it seemed as if the *Fray Bentos* involvement in the battle for Hill 35 was over, but this was not to be the case. In fact, it had only just begun.

Captain Richardson decided to leave the shelter of *Fray Bentos* to prepare the tank's unditching gear with a view to getting it back on the move. Fire from Gallipoli and the surrounding German infantry, now beginning to close-in on the stranded tank, proved to be too intense and, not wishing to ride his luck and leave his men leaderless, he gave-up his task and climbed back into the comparative safety of the tank. Private Braedy and Sergeant Missen also attempted to get to the unditching gear but Braedy was killed and Missen returned to the interior of the tank.

The 8th Seaforth Highlanders and 7th Cameron Highlanders, 44th Brigade, 15th Division had now moved closer and attempted to rush the strongpoint, but were driven off by the heavy fire leaving *Fray Bentos* in a vulnerable position about 500 yards in advance of the British Line. The infantry took heavy casualties and were relieved later in the day by the 10th Scottish Rifles and the 9th Black Watch, the latter receiving orders to attack Gallipoli at 1.30 a.m. the following morning. This they did, failing in their objective and gaining no more than 100 yards of ground at a cost of one officer killed and 50 other ranks killed or wounded. If that wasn't enough for the Black Watch, their battalion headquarters took a direct hit from a shell during the attack, resulting in their headquarters' staff losing 12 men killed and nine wounded.[1]

In the meantime, the crew of *Fray Bentos* had stayed with her, hoping for relief and the opportunity to become mobile again. However, the Germans then started to move forward from their recaptured position around Gallipoli towards the British trenches, but they had reckoned without the crew in *Fray Bentos*. Having missed the chance of restarting their machine they were still active and spoiling for a fight. Although the tank was out of action, its armament wasn't, and the crew decided to put it to good use. Time and time again, the fury of their fire brought the advancing enemy to a stop. *Fray Bentos* was now virtually an isolated fort in the middle of No-Man's Land - a strongpoint in its own right. Try as they may, all through the heat of the August afternoon, the Germans could make no impression on the isolated machine, and whenever they closed they were made aware of the risk they were taking by the deadly stream of fire from the stranded *Fray Bentos*. Its resolute crew, under the redoubtable Captain Richardson, were determined to discharge their duty to the full.

To add more difficulties, a new threat had to be taken into consideration. The British infantry, assuming that *Fray Bentos* was in enemy hands, was also firing at it. Things looked pretty grim and it seemed ironical to Captain Richardson that, having come so far, he and his crew could now be consigned to eternity by the combined efforts of both their own and the enemy's guns.

"Adversity produces the hero", so says the adage and Sergeant H. Missen, a 26-year-old professional soldier described as "steady as a rock", volunteered to get back to British lines to let everyone know that the *Fray Bentos* crew was alive and kicking and still in command of both the tank and the situation they found themselves in. Even though spotted by enemy snipers, Sergeant Missen managed to cross No-Man's Land to ensure that the infantry, who were astounded to hear that the tank garrison was still British and still in action, picked other targets, and a white flag was hung from one of the *Fray Bentos* ports to signal that she was still manned by her original occupiers.

With the British infantry now selecting other targets, Captain Richardson had one thing less to worry about. He had already dismissed all thoughts of escape. Lieutenant Hill was in a weakened state and others in the crew were the worse for wear but *Fray Bentos* was not short of ammunition and there was sufficient water and rations to carry on for days. He therefore steeled himself to hold the vital ground surrounding his improvised redoubt and see what transpired.

The afternoon heat of the first day waned and as night fell on the Flemish hillside the ever watchful crew prepared for all eventualities. They kept alert, always returning steady fire and taking the offensive at any signs of movement in or around the Gallipoli fortifications. They took it in turns to rest and cat-nap, and maintained a sentry on strict alert all through the night. Enemy patrols probed continuously but, like 'Horatius defending the Bridge', *Fray Bentos* stood its lonely ground between the lines.

Came the dawn of another day, came the first of the German attempts to unbalance them, but the men in the little fort, standing proud in the open before Gallipoli, held firm and responded to every assault with a withering fire. Whatever the imprisoned crew were called upon to do, they did with a determined grit. Captain Richardson was proud of them, and rightly so.

As the sun rose, it brought with it the thoughts of relief, but the sound of rifle-fire and machine-guns soon belied that thought. Nevertheless, daylight relaxed frayed nerves a little even though it exposed to the crew all that which was opposing them. Lieutenant Hill was in a bad way and it was essential he soon received medical help. Captain Richardson considered abandoning the tank to return with his men to the British line, but against this was the sure knowledge that, if they gave up now, the Germans would surge through unimpeded.

The second day, 23rd August, passed very slowly, or so it seemed to the crew. A little excitement had been aroused in them when they became aware of the attack by the 9th Black Watch but their hopes were shattered when this failed. Several times, German probes initiated from the smoking bunker and trenches were repulsed with blistering fire at great loss to the aggressors, and the British infantry further back now had the correct targets following Sergeant Missen's courageous mission the previous evening.

On the night, of 23rd, Richardson surveyed his band of warriors and recognised the resolve in them all. They were behind him in his determination not to cede this vital position. He wondered if he could get them through another night. He had the ammunition to hold on but was his own obstinacy threatening their safety?

He had considered a night escape before the crew's morale began to wilt and cause despair, but his longer view was to hold on while he could. The Germans would find it difficult to by-pass or take his little redoubt so, while he perceived his crew were with him, he would stand and fight.

The second night began quietly, suggesting the enemy had gone to ground to prepare for a new day, but when slight movements were heard on the roof of the tank the Captain knew something was afoot, maybe a new tactic to smoke them out perhaps? He rapidly issued instructions and all apertures in the tank were opened and with every available weapon to-hand the crew blasted away in all directions in the engulfing darkness. The enemy scattered quickly, taking their wounded with them.

Back in their own dug-outs and the safety of their trenches the enemy blasted back a furious barrage of armour-piercing bullets and this time *Fray Bentos* was out of luck. Some of the bullets penetrated the armour plating and flew all around the restricted interior wounding all but one within. Captain Richardson now accepted things were going against him and that continued assaults by the enemy could only result in both *Fray Bentos* and its crew being taken.

Time passed slowly and with dawn of the third day making its fitful appearance, Captain Richardson hoped that at least some form of relief must come. His crew looked all in. They had slept fitfully and the food, and more importantly, the water, were running out. The all-pervading stench of oil and cordite filled the tank's interior, but still the crew were determined to hang on. Never for once was Gallipoli out of their sights nor, come to that, were the enemy casualties littering the ground between it and *Fray Bentos*, poor consolation maybe but at least a visible indication that their efforts were not entirely in vain.

With the coming of the night, Captain Richardson decided enough was enough. The wounded needed urgent help and he felt a fourth night in the isolation of the tank would be asking too much. They had done their duty, now was the time to hand on the banner to others so, at 9 p.m. on 24th August, he gave the order to retire. Quietly, under the cover of night during a lull in the firing, hatches were opened and he and his gallant crew hauled themselves out. Undefeated, they crawled back across the 500 yards of battered landscape to the British lines where admiring hands were ready with badly needed assistance. They left the smouldering wreck of *Fray Bentos* to its fate, with small parties of enemy already filtering around it.[2] She had done her duty and made a name for herself in the records of the British Army.

The stand made by *Fray Bentos* and her crew would become a by-word for dogged resistance. After having eliminated one strongpoint on the slopes of Hill 35, they had faced-off the second, Gallipoli, a well-fortified, strategically-sited German position, and had frustrated a marauding force from early 22nd August through to 9 p.m. on the 24th, a torturous period in excess of sixty hours.[3] It had been an epic resistance by a small, determined tank-crew. A magnificent feat by any standard, and the British infantry involved on the hill would have had occasion to remember, and to be grateful to the crew of Tank *F.41.*

Casualties from the crew of nine totalled two officers and six other ranks wounded and one other rank, Private Ernest H. Braedy, killed. Captain Richardson and Lieutenant Hill were awarded the Military Cross. Sergeant Missen and Gunner Morrey were each awarded the D.C.M., and Gunners Hayton, Arthurs, Budd and Binley the Military Medal. Private Braedy is commemorated on the Memorial to the Missing in Tyne Cot Cemetery, Passchendaele.

The overall attack did not succeed in its objectives and the action reports from the tank commanders all tell a sorry tale:

F.42 and *F.47* took direct hits at the Starting Point and were put out of action.

F.47 (Foam) at Spree Farm. She received a direct hit while lining-up at Starting Point, smashing her rear left sponson, but moved off at zero hour then, after 50 yards, was hit again, wounding the officer and five crew-members. The officer ordered her to be cleared and stripped of her guns before being abandoned.

F.43 ditched just behind *Fray Bentos* on the latter's approach to Somme Farm.

F.46, ditched itself when returning to support the infantry who were held up in a shell hole by enemy fire. This tank could not be unditched and the crew, on leaving it, were taken prisoner.

F.45 ditched near Gallipoli and an attempt by *F.49* to tow her out failed. *F.49* with the wounded and the Lewis guns of *F.45* on board and in the vicinity of Gallipoli where the infantry were digging-in, handed over three Lewis guns before returning to Spree Farm, then received a direct hit and sank in the mud.

F.48 received a direct hit before reaching Starting Point but managed to move off at Zero – and ditched. Eventually she managed to move off at 8 a.m., then received orders to return to the rallying point where a fresh crew took over and took her to Pond Farm. She returned to the rallying point after two hours of action after the infantry had established their positions.

F.45 (Fiducia), sister tank to *F.47* in the attack, ditched near Gallipoli and although an attempt was made to tow her out, it failed. Her wounded and Lewis Guns were taken aboard *F.49* which returned to Spree Farm. *F.45* was abandoned near Gallipoli, a long, long way from her designated target, Schuler Gallery.

Captain Richardson's action report of *Fray Bentos* tends to understate what he the crew and their tank had been through:

I have the honour to report that during the operations of the morning August 22nd, 1917, in which my section (No. 9) were assisting the 61st. Division, I attached myself to 2/Lieut. G. Hill, in charge of Male Tank F.41, whose objectives were SOMME - GALLIPOLI - MARTHA HOUSE and KANSAS HOUSE.

We left the point of deployment immediately behind Spree Farm at 4.40 a.m. - 5 minutes before ZERO hour. Immediately on ZERO hour, the enemy put down a heavy Crump barrage, which we got through successfully, with the exception of two holes blown behind the right outer Track-Adjuster. We proceeded by way of SOMME coming under heavy M.G. fire from that direction. We engaged it with our left 6-Pounder, and the firing ceased.

At 5.30. a.m Tank F.43 was working immediately on our right as per operation orders (the Lieutenant-Colonel Commanding 'F' Battalion notes in the action reports "I am of the opinion that Captain Richardson is mistaken in saying that he saw F. 43 on his right."), About this time we also saw a "C" Battalion Tank on our immediate right. About 5.45 a.m. we came under heavy M.G. fire from GALLIPOLI and vicinity. Whilst engaging this target Mr. Hill was struck in the neck by the fragments of a bullet and was temporarily put out of action; it was at this juncture, whilst changing places, that the Tank became ditched. Two attempts were made to put on the unditching gear, but proved fruitless owing to the enemy's concentrated M.G. and rifle fire. Whilst in this position we successfully engaged the machine-guns at GALLIPOLI Farm with the 6-Pounder gun. About this time our own infantry, of whom we had seen very little, began to go back leaving us isolated, the enemy followed closely up but were checked by our 6-Pounder and Lewis gun fire. We stayed in this position until 9 p.m. of the evening of the 24th inst., being unable to unditch the Tank owing to snipers and machine-guns. During this time we were sniped at by both our own people and the enemy, but managed to stop our own people by showing a white rag through one of our Portholes.

During the action each member of the crew received wounds. Lance Corporal Braedy lost his life whilst fitting the unditching gear under terrific M.G. fire.

Great gallantry was shown by Gunner W. Morrey, who carried on though hit in the arm and leg.

Owing to the barrage it was extremely difficult to pick up land marks, and direction was successfully kept by means of the Chart supplied and by R.O., and the Mariner's Compass in the Tank. After leaving the Tank we reported to the nearest infantry Unit - 9th Black Watch, who promised to place a covering detachment to keep the enemy from entering the Tank. We placed the Lewis Guns at the disposal of the 9th Black Watch. I reported this to Brigade Headquarters at MILL COTT.

Strangely enough, Captain Richardson makes no mention of Sergeant Missen's gallant trip from Fray Bentos back to the British line. The Battalion Commander's report notes it thus:

Sergeant Missen got out of the Tank and made his way to our line to prevent our infantry shooting anyone out of the Tank, as the Tank was being sniped at by both the enemy and our infantry.

Sergeant H. Missen's own report on the action, as unassuming and as straightforward as the man himself, was as follows:

We got on well after starting and we got to GALLIPOLI. I am sure it was Gallipoli, C Battn had a tank stopped just on the slope on our right and we went on over the ridge by some buildings. Mr Harding's tank was on our left flank about 500 yards off us. I fired a 6-pounder at a concrete shed in front of Mr Harding's tank and range was 400.

We got into a very deep soft place and went in sideways and just at that moment Mr Hill fell back off his seat hit, Capt Richardson got on the seat to relieve him but he was foul of the controls and before the driver could do anything she was right in and ditched. Budd and Morrey were hit at the same time.

Budd was unconscious for about 2 hours. Mr Hill hit in head and neck, Morrey arm and leg. I got out of right sponson door to put on one side of the unditching gear but I heard bullets hitting the tank and saw some Bosch about 30 yards off firing at me, I got in again.

Braedy had got out of the other side to help me, and they shot him, and he fell under the side of the tank that was sinking. Arthurs said he was dead.

We kept on firing and killed several Bosch close to the tank, we had expected the infantry to come at any time.

We had a lot of trouble with the Lewis. The Bosch were in an old trench close under the front of the tank and we could not get the

Lewis on them owing to the angle of the tank, but we shot them easily with a rifle out of the revolver flap in the cab. There were some infantry behind us but they did not look like coming on.

Captain Richardson told me to go back and warn the infantry not to shoot us as we should sooner or later have to clear out of the tank. We were all getting stiff from wounds.

I got out of the right sponson door and crawled back to the infantry They were the Gordons. I stopped there for about an hour expecting the others to come. I heard a few shots as if the Bosch were sniping at the people coming from the tank.

I kept looking and then saw what I thought was two Officers going back to my right rear. I thought they were Capt Richardson and Mr Hill and went after them but lost them in the broken ground and the infantry could tell me nothing of them.

I went across to Rat Farm but there were only dead there and I went on up to Wieltje to report. When I left the casualties were:

Mr. Hill w, head and neck.

Capt Richardson w, arm, slight.

Braedy. Dead

Budd, w, head but carried on when he came round.

Morrey w, L arm and leg.

Arthurs w R arm.

Hayton w head (slight).

Binley not touched.

Remained beating off constant Bosch attacks till night of 24th, when withdrawn bring 6 pr: locks and Lewis guns.

No arms nor maps left in tank."

Notes:

1. After many fierce encounters, the 55th (West Lancashire) Division finally captured Gallipoli on 20th September, 1917.

2. The fate of Fray Bentos is not known. Another tank, named Fray Bentos II was captured during the Battle of Cambrai in November 1918 and shown to Wilhelm II at Bad Kreuznach during a showing of the German 'spoils of war'.

3. The farms Somme and Gallipoli were rebuilt near their original sites after the war but the bunker fortifications were removed in the post-war years before the Belgian Government put a stop to the destruction of military concrete structures.

The photograph, taken from the edge of the farm complex which was the centre of the Gallipoli strongpoint during the war years, shows the relative position of one of its sister strongpoints on the hill, Somme, nestling on the downward slope of Hill 35. Fray Bentos was ditched in a position to the left of Somme halfway up the slope towards Gallipoli, having silenced the Somme garrison while passing it on the left on its way up. The British line was approximately 200 yards behind Somme. The farm that was Gallipoli was rebuilt closer to the road than the original and traces of the footings are noticeable at the back of today's farm.

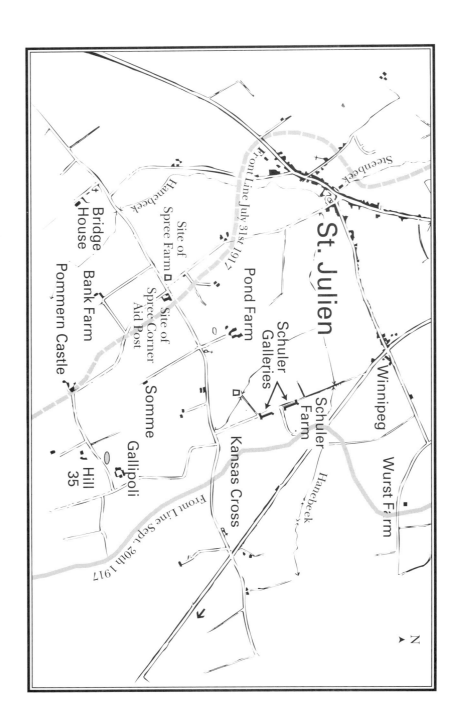

St. Julien

Steenbeek

Front Line July 31st 1917

Hanebeek

Bridge House

Site of Spree Farm

Bank Farm

Site of Spree Corner Aid Post

Pommern Castle

Somme

Pond Farm

Schuler Galleries

Schuler Farm

Winnipeg

Wurst Farm

Kansas Cross

Hanebeek

Gallipoli

Hill 35

Front Line Sept. 20th 1917

N

10
THE LIVERPOOL IRISH AT SCHULER GALLERIES
Pond Farm area, September 1917

S CHULER FARM, LYING JUST TO THE NORTH-EAST of Pond Farm on the Zonnebeke–Langemarck road, was of great tactical importance to the Germans as the British attacks progressed from the flat meadows beyond Wieltje, moved north of St. Julien and began the tortuous ascent of the low ridges *en route* to the main target of the Passchendaele ridge during the Third Battle of Ypres. This importance was determined by the field of fire it commanded and the fact that its system of underground chambers could afford protection for large groups of defenders. On the eastern side of the track, running south-east to north-west in front of the farm the Germans had constructed a concrete gallery with machine-gun emplacements branching-off on the western edges. These were the famous Schuler Galleries. When the Lancastrians of the 55th (West Lancs) Division finally crushed the resistance here in September 1917, after ferocious close combat, over one thousand enemy soldiers were captured, many of whom had been taking refuge in these underground galleries. Twice during the summer campaign of 1917, this division saw action at this position, in the late July at the start of the Third Battle of Ypres and again during the September battles of the Menin Road when success would mark their efforts.

An account by Second-Lieutenant R. B. Hodson of the 8th Battalion Liverpool Irish (164th Brigade, 55th Division) who took part in both attacks on the position well describes the securing of the Schuler Galleries in September 1917.

Hodson, a 30-year-old former accountant from Aintree, Liverpool, had risen from the ranks after enlisting in June 1915. His narrative is a sound description of the advance. On receiving his commission, he had been pleased to find himself in the Liverpool (Irish). As a fervent Roman Catholic, he surmised many of the men would also be co-religionist and would be something basic and sustaining to share in the dark days ahead. He had seen action both at Guillemont on the Somme in 1916 and in the Ypres Salient early in 1917. He had acquitted himself well and, as gleaned from letters and documents, he was a well-respected officer.

His narrative begins at the opening of the Third Battle of Ypres. As Platoon Officer in 'C' Company. The battalion concentrated in Liverpool Trench and Congreve Walk assembly trenches around Wieltje from which the division would 'jump off' in the early hours of 31st July. The Irish were not to be used until 8.30 a.m. when the 164th Brigade would support and mop-up following attacks by other brigades in the division.

The objectives were the fortified farms and pill-boxes between Wieltje and St. Julien with the 15th (Scottish) Division on the right, moving on Zonnebeke. Second Lieutenant Hodson's report of 3rd August to his Commanding Officer states:

Sir

I have the honour to place before you my report of the fighting on 31st July 1917.

As 'moppers up' to the 2/5th Lancashire Fusiliers, my Company (C Coy) left the jumping off trench at 8.30 am.

Our advance was good until we approached a point about C23.b.80.40. Here we came under a very heavy barrage of enemy guns. Moving quickly we soon reached the Black Line at Spree Farm at 9.35 am. In Capricorn Trench we found the 1/10th King's (Scottish) Liverpool Regiment where a number or our own wounded were seen. A heavy fire from snipers and machine-guns was playing around us at the time. While waiting for our own barrage to lift (at 10.10 am) we suffered some heavy casualties. I found that this was due to the snipers located in the row of trees to the right of Capricorn (8 in number). I directed my Lewis guns and rifle fire onto these trees. Fire had a good effect. The snipers had claimed 2 Officers of my Company, the Company Sergeant Major besides several other ranks. Most of the men lost on the Black Line were a result of this fire. I personally reported the matter and the action I had taken to Officer Commanding the 2/5th Lancashire Fusiliers. Following barrage as closely as possible, I moved my men on to the object under a heavy enemy fire of shells, machine-guns and rifles. We passed Pond Farm which was being cleared of the enemy and on to Hindu Cottage. Here, one of our tanks was doing excellent work and his covering fire allowed us to move across the open to machine-gun emplacements at D13.a.80.30 to D13.a.60.80.

The emplacements were giving a hard fight. A tank was summoned up and together we cleared the place of the enemy. The deeper dugouts were bombed and a quantity of prisoners taken. Many German dead were found. Whilst searching the H.Q. dugout a bundle of papers was found burning on the stove but could not be retrieved. It appeared I was in his Battalion Headquarters. Their emplacements were found to be well preserved, with very little damage done to emplacements. There was also little apparent damage done to his wire which looked very thick and strong. Our guns had not had the desired effect here and it was fortunate we had a tank on hand to help with our task.

From the emplacements we moved on to Schuler Farm, the hedges around the Farm were thick and seemingly undamaged. It was from this cover that O. C. 'A' Coy (Captain Bodel) and myself re-organised our men. (Captain Bodel was killed later in the day by shell-fire at Schuler Farm.)

Schuler was searched and found to be unoccupied. We found three dead horses at the farm and from this I concluded the enemy had been moving his guns away for they were heavy horses. Eventually we succeeded in reaching the Kansas Cross-Winnipeg Road and I decided to take up a line at this point just in front of the farm.

During this time we were continually subjected to sniper fire and machine-gun fire which appeared to come from our flanks and to our front from just across the road already mentioned.

A message was sent to H.Q. at 2.30 p.m. giving our position. Whilst we were making good our line, four enemy planes flew over observing where we were. From this I concluded that they were seeking information to be used in a particular sector.

Second-Lieutenant Hodson was correct in his conclusion. Several different sources refer to the sterling work done by those enemy flyers who had been operating over the ridge for several hours and reporting back. One of their messages must have startled the German local command when they observed units from the 55th Division sector cross the main Zonnebeke Road and ascend the lower slopes of the Ridge reaching as far as two of their major strongpoints, Aviatik and Wurst Farms.

These were in fact Hodson's and Bodel's companies, who evicted the garrison at Wurst Farm after a fierce fight and began to fortify the surrounds in strength. Nevertheless, pressure from the enemy who had now begun to recover his nerve, intensified as accurate information got back to them. Massive counter-attacks were quickly organised and implemented from high ground around Gravenstafel.

From several points along the ridge, the German storm-troopers hammered away at the 55th and 39th Divisions, fresh troops against tired men who had been slogging it out all day. The 39th Division, particularly about St. Julien, wilted visibly under the onslaught and were thrown back along the banks of the Steenbeek, with a battalion of Hertfordshires practically disappearing in the day's fighting. With their left flank now bending sharply and non-existent in some places, the 55th Division, the Liverpool Irish particularly, were hit hard from several directions at once. The defenders at Wurst Farm, well over a hundred strong, fought to a standstill before their threat was nullified and only a handful of survivors returned to their lines in the late afternoon.

Second-Lieutenant Hodson sheltering in a shell hole in front of Schuler Farm, sensing the deteriorating situation, continued:

> We noticed our flanks falling back, so at 2.40 p.m. we took up a new position back at the recently won M.G. emplacements (The Galleries).
>
> Our Brigade Major (164th) came up and I gave him the full situation. Acting on his orders we adjusted slightly and got behind what had once been the enemy's front wire now in our rear. This gave us a good field of fire. I was also reinforced with 3 guns and crews from

the 164th M.G. Coy. We did not have very long to wait. At 3.30 pm the enemy came on in force immediately to our front. We held our positions as ordered until all our ammunition ran out, then with the remainder of my men fought a fighting retreat back to the Black Line near Spree Farm and Capricorn Trench. When we arrived I reported to the Senior Officer on the spot, the O.C. 1/4th Loyal North Lancashire Regiment.

Thus Hodson covers his contribution in countering the enemy attacks on Schuler Farm. He would be mentioned in dispatches for his day's work. His efforts, and those of others along this fluid front, had hampered the Germans, buying valuable time for those back on the Black Line to construct a new line to fight on. German losses had been heavy but as the remnants of the Liverpool Irish limped back across the shell-torn landscape they might have thought of Guillemont, where likewise they were forced to give back what they had earned because of eroded flanks.

On the Black Line itself, the Battalion's Adjutant, Captain C. Jones and the Commanding Officer of the 2/5th Lancashire Fusiliers, Lieutenant-Colonel B. Best-Dunkley, had worked wonders in erecting fresh defences and bringing order to the chaos caused by the enemy counter-attacks. It would not be untoward to attribute the halting of the German advance in the sector to the leadership and industry of those two officers.

In the mid-afternoon, both were seriously wounded by the same shell-explosion. Jones spent several weeks in hospital and his report on the proceedings implies, in his opinion, that the shell was a British 'short'. Lieutenant-Colonel Best-Dunkley died a few days later at Proven. He was awarded a posthumous Victoria Cross for his command of the early attack when his skills and leadership extricated the Fusiliers from a serious situation when in danger of being bogged down. An extract from the *London Gazette* No. 30272, dated 4th September 1917 records the following:

For most conspicuous bravery and devotion to duty when in command of his battalion, the leading waves of which, during the attack, became disorganised by reason of rifle and machine-gun fire at close range from positions which were believed to be in our hands.

Lt. Col. Best-Dunkley dashed forward, rallied his leading waves, and personally led them to the assault of these positions, which, despite heavy losses, were captured.

He continued to lead his battalion until all their objectives had been gained. Had it not been for this officer's gallant and determined action it is doubtful if the left of the brigade would have reached its objectives. Later in the day, when our position was threatened, he collected his battalion headquarters, led them to the attack, and beat off the advancing enemy.[1]

Second-Lieutenant Hodson completes his report with a couple of sharply observed details:

Whilst falling back we were subjected to an incessantly accurate barrage. we had commented on its efficiency, but I had been aware of the fact, that when his infantry approached us he lifted his barrage at a precise signal from them. This was a small white light, in my opinion fired from his leading section. His subsequent fire was precisely on the line of these lights. When at the Galleries the lights were fired directly at our rifle pits, within a minute his fire was within yards of our position.

From Black Line I was instructed to rejoin 164 Brigade at Congreve Walk, Wieltje and report to Captain Monks of the 8th Battalion. This I did with my men on August 1st at 4.15 pm. We then held Lone Trench and New John Street until relieved officially on August 2nd. At point D13.b.20.70, there was a strong brick-built structure. The top of this was shaped like a beehive. This could have been a M.G. emplacement, but more probably an observation post. It was in very good condition.

I have the honour Sir, to be your Obedient Servant.

R. W. Hodson. August 3rd 1917.

Hodson must have written-up his report on the action after arriving in the St. Omer billeting area following the relief by the 36th (Ulster) Division. In a reflective mood, he may well have considered what the efforts on 31st July had cost. True, they had smashed a formidable defensive line and before counter-attacks and the changing weather had brought them to a halt, they had inflicted a serious loss on the enemy's men and materials. Some 600 prisoners had been accounted for in the 55th Divisional area alone. On the other hand, the debit column was bleak. Of eighteen officers of the Liverpool Irish who had gone into action at 8.30 a.m. only two were to return unscathed in the afternoon, Second-Lieutenant Fenn and Hodson himself. 310 other ranks had become casualties in a sector barely half-a-mile long and a quarter-of-a-mile wide. It had been a savage loss and the 160 other survivors of the battalion who concentrated around St. Omer on 3rd August must have breathed a sigh of relief at their good luck.

The conditions on the battlefield were already changing as the last of the Liverpool Irish left it. The rain hammered down, seeming to side with the enemy. Both sides settled down for a watchful but wary night as the trenches and shell-holes filled with water. Mud changed to slime and everyone concerned fought hard against disappointment and discouragement. Conditions were enough to break the spirit of all but the most stoic.

The division was given over a month's rest, as was necessary to recover from its exertions on 31st July. It was 12th September before it was on the move back to Ypres.

Hodson, now a Captain, took command of 'A' Company, a post previously held by his old friend Captain Bodel who died in the action at Schuler.[2]

On 31st July, the 164th Brigade would be involved yet again in the very same sector as the next stage of the battle developed. The attack was planned for the early hours of 20th September and the overall offensive would come to be known as the Battle of the Menin Road.

Whilst their objective remained Schuler Farm and its protecting Galleries, the fighting that had continued since their departure had advanced the line a little so that now the jumping-off trenches would be slightly in front of Pond Farm. Captain Hodson's company would have about 500 yards of No-Man's Land to cross to the Schuler position. Pond Farm, commanding the approaches from Wieltje and St. Julien, had been a very sensitive point in the German defences and had been strongly held. Now it was secure in British hands having cost the 36th and the 61st Divisions over 800 casualties between them.

Transferred to 'D' Company, Captain Hodson doubtless viewed the prospect of another attack across the same ground, and with the same objectives, with some trepidation. However, according to an official account, enemy counter-fire was not so heavy or so intense as that encountered in late July, even though machine-gun and sniper fire was directed onto the Liverpool Irish from the farm ahead and the Hanebeek stream on the left. This caused a temporary check to Hodson and his leading platoons as they went to ground. In doing so they lost their protecting barrage which, on a rigid timetable, lifted on cue, and moved-off to the other side of the Zonnebeke Road. The enemy at Schuler swiftly exploited the predicament of the Liverpool Irish and poured fire into them as they closed on the Galleries. Not to be denied, and admirably led by Captain Hodson and Monks, the platoons tore into the Galleries and in the words of the regimental history:

> The Liverpool Irish rallied and swept like an angry flood over the shell-holes and took up position in front of the Galleries, shooting down or bayonetting the remaining Germans who refused to surrender.

Resistance was still unyielding from the emplacements, but by bringing up his reserve platoons and employing them swiftly from the left-flank, Hodson was able to report at 7.15 a.m. that the Schuler Galleries were once more in British hands. A hundred prisoners had been taken and the next few hours were spent in reorganising and consolidating the line facing the farm. Fire from there was still fierce and the narrow stretch of open ground between the adversaries was swept by a murderous hail of bullets making the cost of an attack prohibitive, not that Hodson felt he had enough men to attempt it. Securing the Galleries had cost the Liverpool Irish nearly 150 casualties, including 50 dead, so these depleted platoons would have a very difficult task indeed. It was decided to wait until the early hours of 21st September when it was judged that the enemy defence might not be so alert. So it proved. Precisely at 4.30 a.m., a specially-selected platoon, led by Second-Lieutenant Allerton, one of Hodson's young platoon officers, moved speedily to the farm buildings and after a short, sharp action, took it from a stunned and weary garrison. Many enemy dead and wounded were found in and around the farm. The work of the 164th Brigade came to an end in this particular campaign with the capture of Schuler Farm. For the second time the Liverpool Irish had done its work well and this time there would be no repeat of July. It was theirs to keep and would be so until they were relieved by the 59th (North Midland) Division and moved back to the Watou area for a rest. A new front was tenuously formed from Kansas Cross, the crossroads where the Wieltje-Gravenstafel road crossed the Zonnebeke-Langemarck road to the Hanebeek stream, but it would not be needed. The enemy had finally decided not to contest this sector. He had relinquished it for good and had withdrawn up the ridge to new positions around Gravenstafel and the Abraham Heights. As for Captain Hodson who had been so prominent in capturing the redoubtable Galleries, his war came to an abrupt and painful end in the late afternoon of 20th September.

Standing with a small group of his men and some captured German officers, a sudden burst of fire scattered the group and Hodson was hit in the face and immediately fell to the ground. Two members of his company left accounts of his wounding and subsequent removal to the aid post:

Corporal Parry No 7 platoon:

I was with Captain Hodson at the storming of the Galleries. Everyone was excited and elated. As the Captain was interrogating some German prisoners prior to sending them down to Wieltje, we were fired on and he was hit in the jaw and face and fell.

Lance Corporal Ward. No. 1 Platoon:

After we had taken the concrete galleries with the bayonet, I was ordered to escort a badly limping German officer back to the aid post set up near Pond Farm. On the way back, I glanced down and saw Captain Hodson near the galleries, lying in a shallow shell hole. He was desperately trying to right himself. I propped him up on his own pack to ease the bleeding which was plentiful and tried without much success to patch him up with his own first aid kit. Before returning to the galleries I called upon two stretcher bearers working nearby and stayed with Captain Hodson until he was temporarily patched up and taken down in the direction of Pond Farm. I was very sad to see him go he was very well respected, but he did look in a very bad way.

So Captain Hodson left the field of battle for the last time having completed almost twelve months in the dreaded Ypres Salient He was taken down the line of casualty clearing stations and, in the first week of October, he arrived on the coast, north of Boulogne at No 5 Red Cross Hospital, Wimereux. Here he was to undergo several intricate, painful and not very successful operations in a bid to rebuild his shattered jaw.

The wounds he received at Schuler Galleries continued to be a problem for him for a long time after the war and the treatment he received was painful and lengthy. It was just before the Armistice in November 1918 that the military medical board judged his injuries to be so severe that his further active service in the field would be out of the question. He was discharged as medically unfit for military life on 2nd November 1918.

His wounds prevented a full return to health and his hospital appointment calendar grew longer and longer as the consultants fought a grim battle to ease his daily pain. By virtue of his resilient character and his determination not to cede to his injury, he strived for a time to return to his former work and resume the natural order of life. In the summer of 1922 his health had improved somewhat, and he married his long-time fiancée, They settled down to leading an ordinary life together, buying a small house in the Liverpool suburb of Maghull, and planning for the future like any other newly-married couple.

Unfortunately, the fates which ordain such things had already decided that the destiny which had avoided him that traumatic day at Schuler Farm five years before would now reach out to him for the reckoning. He suffered a painful relapse and a fierce infection set in. He was rushed to hospital for an urgent operation but did not withstand the effects and sadly died in March 1923 at a premature 36 years of age. He was buried at Our Lady's Roman Catholic Church at Lydiate on 10th April 1923.

This gallant officer had escaped the terrors of the ferocious and bitter fighting in the Ypres Salient, but fate had decided he would not be free from the shadows cast at Schuler. At his funeral, his employer commented to his widow, "Bitter as the blow must be to you, I hope you will have the consolation in remembering that he surely died for his country".

Today, the lie of the land and its features in the battle area, where Captain Hodson and his colleagues suffered are still in place. Pond Farm still sits on the left of the road from Wieltje to Gravenstafel. Spree Farm and the crossroads are no longer there, but Spree Corner calls up echoes of overworked medical officers of the Lancastrian Division and the redoubtable Captain Ferguson of the Rifle Brigade two years before Passchendaele. Bridge House and its cemetery, a small enclosure by Western Front standards, paying tribute to some of the dead from the nearby aid posts, houses only a fraction of the men who fell locally. Most of those who died here are remembered on the Menin Gate Memorial to the Missing at Ypres, as the fighting over a long period so pulverised this area that many local graves became one with the earth. North-east of Pond Farm, across a slightly undulating meadow, is Schuler Farm with the dusty track running before it covering the empty chambers of the infamous Schuler Galleries. This whole area saw more than its fair share of fighting during the war and it will be found mentioned in numerous divisional, brigade and battalion histories. Nature and the local Belgian farming community have reclaimed it, and it is now difficult to imagine that this peaceful agricultural area of Flanders records a piece of military history.

Notes:

1. Lt.-Col. Best-Dunkley died on 5th August 1917. He is buried at Mendinghem British Cemetery, Proven, Belgium, Plot III, Row D, Grave I.

2. The body of Captain F. E. Bodel M.C., 8th Battalion Liverpool (Irish) was never recovered. He is commemorated on the Menin Gate Memorial to the Missing at Ypres.

3. Captain Hodson's dramatic accounts of the actions at Schuler Farm and Galleries are from the private papers left to his nephew, Mr P. W. Leigh of Twickenham, Middlesex.

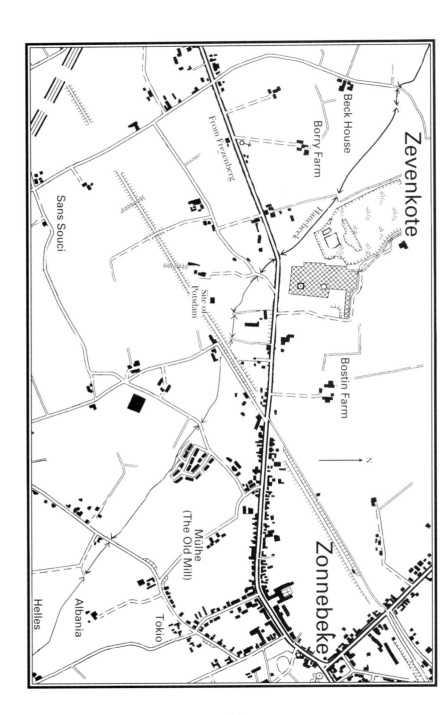

Zevenkote

Beck House

Borry Farm

From Frezenberg

Hanebeek

Sans Souci

Site of
Potsdam

Bostin Farm

N

Mühle
(The Old Mill)

Zonnebeke

Helles

Albania

Tokio

11
THE O'DONNELL TWINS
Ypres 1917

S OMEONE OF LITERARY NOTE once observed that: "There is one thing worse than not having a brother, and that is losing a brother". An understandable emotion, but how much more painful that loss when a twin dies, especially within the maelstrom of war. The Great War period of 1914–1918 is littered with examples of brothers serving together, or near one another, and deep must have been the pain for a lone survivor.

Few seem to fit this emotive profile so neatly as the O'Donnell twins, Jack and Tom, two young Irish-Australians who wore the Australian cap badge as proudly as any Anzac. But what part would the little Belgian town of Ypres, of which they had probably never heard previously, play in their personal odyssey? Jack and Tom would look out for each other when their respective battalions were near enough to do so, but battle conditions usually prevailed against them.

The twin brothers were typical of the many thousands of young Irishmen who had emigrated to the vast new continent across the globe to seek a new life. Although they both worked in the local bank at Tullow, County Carlow, where their father had a senior job, the prospects offered in Australia were too good to miss. Jack arrived in Adelaide under an assisted immigrant scheme in 1911, followed shortly afterwards by Tom. They met up with their uncle, Patrick Glynn, who had vouched for them, and who had already settled and entered local politics. Banking seemed the obvious profession again, and their previous experience stood them in good stead. The two 23-year-olds could look forward to a bright future, but a black cloud was about to blight their hopes. The Great War erupted in 1914, and life for the O'Donnell twins, as for so many the world over, would never be the same again.

Jack enlisted on 26th August 1914, one of the original thousand riflemen that constituted the 10th local battalion of the Australian Infantry Force. Only thirty of these thousand men would survive the war. Jack O'Donnell would be one of them.

Tom soon joined his brother in the ranks of the volunteers. Australia was vast in space but small in populace, with no tradition of militia, although small parties had previously gone to help the Mother Country in the Egyptian and South African campaigns. The rapid rush of recruits, though welcome, soon resembled a quart trying to fit in a pint pot, as hoards of men clamoured to the colours. Australia's small, and so far leisured military operation, was overwhelmed by this surge of eager warriors. Tom was duly posted to the 50th Battalion, which would be part of the new 4th Australian Division, being made ready for service.

Australia sent 300,000 men overseas, 60,000 of whom fell on foreign soil, sombre figures for the new dominion. Exactly the same proportion of the whole, 20%, were men of Irish extraction. Men the world over saw the Great War as a chance to escape a humdrum existence for adventure in foreign parts. This, together with the feelings of patriotism, excitement, and the prospect of taking part in a monumental event, made up the irresistible mix that drew men to the army like pins to a magnet.

Egypt awaited the early recruits, including Jack O'Donnell, a tranquil prelude to the heroic glory many would find on the rocky crags of the Gallipoli peninsula in April 1915. Leaving many comrades behind on that sand-swept outcrop, further martyrdom was to follow in European locations whose names ever toll a sombre knell for all Australians: Fromelles, Pozières, Bullecourt and most obscene of all, Passchendaele.

Jack O'Donnell, certainly had a hard war, being badly wounded on Gallipoli, and again at Pozières on the Somme, one of the most pulverising battles ever experienced by man, a veritable mincing machine, in which the Australian infantry took nearly 23,000 casualties, a stunning loss for the units taking part. Jack was very lucky to come out alive, and spent several months in 51st General Hospital at Etaples recovering from his wounds.

At Ypres the following year, 1917, where the fighting along the Menin Road was very severe, the Australians drew on the formidable reputation they had gained for themselves since Gallipoli. Jack O'Donnell, back with the 10th Battalion, was wounded for a third time in Polygon Wood. His wound was serious enough to take him out of the line and into hospital at Le Havre on 4th October 1917, little knowing that very day his comrades had played their part in the fall of a powerful German defence position, the Broodseinde Ridge, and that his closest friends in 'C' Company were preparing to mount a raid on a little copse called Celtic Wood on the eastern slopes of that ridge.[1] As an experienced and well-trusted N.C.O., Jack could have been involved in this exercise, had the fortunes of war not ruled him out. As for his devoted brother Tom, he already lay dead, cut down by machine-gun fire from the Old Mill at Zonnebeke a week before on 28th September.[2]

Chance had put Jack in Polygon Wood on 26th September, unaware that brother Tom was manning the line in front of Zonnebeke, waiting for the whistles to blow. Two days later his company attacked, and Tom died, unaware that the brother he followed across the globe, into the war, was just half a mile away.

Tom had not had an easy time since the 50th Battalion arrived in the Salient. He had experienced his fair share of dangers, and throughout his strong Catholic faith, inherent in Irish soldiery down the ages, stood him in good stead. His service record indicates the type of young man he was:

> Beloved by all his pals for his cheery attitude and his humorous sayings, when facing grave danger and enduring severe hardship. He is listed as being the brother of Jack O'Donnell, serving with the 10th Battalion, one of the few brigade survivors of the original landings at Anzac Cove. He (Jack) has refused a commission, and at this time has been wounded and incapacitated twice.

Tom had written a typically spirited letter to his mother in Ireland as he waited to attack and his thoughts fell on brother Jack, who, as he wrote, was just returning to front-line duty:

26 Sept. 1917

Dear Mother, We are all excited about tomorrow. We 'hop' over at daybreak. We all wonder what our fate will be but are not downhearted. We could not hear Mass today more the pity, but Father Bergin kindly looked us up and 'fixed'* us up for the great day.[3]

I am so glad old Jack is out of it at the moment.

Well dearest mother, I must close. Please do not worry, I'll be alright.

PS Have just heard We do not go over the top tomorrow after all. It will be the day after (28th)

(*administered Holy Communion)

This would be Tom's last letter home, for although he survived the first assault, enemy machine-gunners later struck as this happy young adventurer was patrolling No-Man's Land. He was buried where he fell, in temporary graves with the other casualties of the day. After the war, his remains were transferred to one of the new concentration plots at Aeroplane Cemetery on the Frezenberg Ridge, where he lies today.

A colleague, Sydney Robinson, who had gone over the top with Tom, wrote to his mother in early 1918 in response to her concerns over Tom's death and the location of his grave. Syd was unable to offer her much comfort:

I am afraid that the people who look after the graves of our men near Zonnebeke won't be able to help you now, as the portion of the battlefields we held at the time of old Tom's death is now in the hands of the enemy.

They should have had all the particulars for you months ago. Had dear Father Bergin lived, he would have seen to it for you. I don't know if the Graves Dept. attend to the graves up so close to the line, and Tom's grave was within a few hundred yards of the front line. I am sorry I cannot do more for you.

Jack, left alone to mourn, must have missed his sibling intensely. The rest of his war was permeated with illness and spells in different hospitals, and the Armistice found him ensconced in the Royal Victoria Hospital at Netley, Hampshire.

The O'Donnell twins had come a long way from the halcyon days of youth in County Carlow. They had travelled the vast expanse of Australia, experienced the heat and suffering of Gallipoli and survived the killing fields of the Somme. A muddy martyrdom confronted them under the historic bastion of Ypres, one to lie for all time in his soldier's tomb near the town, and the other to carry his grief and memories back to Australia. After a traumatic period, Jack married a young lady he had met in Dublin. Her family were hardly ecstatic at the prospect of them removing to Australia, but Jack and Esther were finally married in 1926, ten years after they had first met, and a child was born to them in the fullness of time. Whilst in Ireland Jack, who had shown a particular talent for poetry, had a book of verse published, entitled *Songs of an Anzac,* one of which was dedicated to his brother:

To Tom
Now comes cruel Winter blighting every bloom
That decked the little mounds in far-off France,
Which plenteous Nature, so profuse always,
No more enhance. In yonder thicket by the old French mill
Where rose and tulip may no longer grow;
He sleeps - softly through the gathering mist
The North Winds blow.
Around - the shambles of the devastating War
Still thunder on - the never ceasing roar
Of cannon - and below the little hill
The star shells soar.
But here in quietude and stately rest,
Where fell the manhood of a southern clime:
Here lie his mates - remembered with the best
Oh! Brother mine
Do you recall way back on sunny shores
The grand old gum trees by Mcarthy's creek;
The Kookaburras laughing in the trees,
And all the world asleep.
Sometimes I think I hear your merry laugh,
As down the Gully distant hooves draw nigh,

And all around the wondrous tropic night
And starry sky.
But when again the Spring in France shall break,
With scarlet poppy and wild Somme flowers,
Perchance some little skylark's notes shall shake
Departing Winter's stillness in the bowers.
And when the tempest of my life is over,
And night draws nigh may I hope to chance
To sleep as peaceful, when my Spring shall break,
As those who fell for France.[4]

Although at one stage of his career, Jack had tried his hand at farming in South Australia, at the time of his death in 1958, following peritonitis, his occupation was listed as 'Labourer'. He was 68 years of age and is buried at Riverstone, New South Wales. Forty years on, the O'Donnell twins were reunited.

Notes:

1) The Old Mill before Zonnebeke was never rebuilt, but the site is easily found. The sweep of land over which Tom O'Donnell's battalion advanced in September 1917 can be traced immediately in front of it in the direction of Ypres.

2) Tom O'Donnell's grave was destroyed in the heavy shelling that followed the battle. His headstone bears the words 'Believed to be buried in this cemetery'.

3) The story of the Celtic Wood raid in October 1917 which Jack O'Donnell missed, is written up in *Anatomy of a Raid* by Spagnoly/Smith 1991.

4) Father Michael Bergin, a Missionary Jesuit and the padre of the 50th Battalion A.I.F., came from Roscrea. Ireland and had never been to Australia. While working in the missions of Egypt and Syria, he met up with the Australian Light Horse. He was accepted by them as padre and received his commission on Anzac Beach, Gallipoli in April 1915. It was said of him "If an angel ever walked among men... it was he". Two weeks after giving Holy Communion to Tom O'Donnell and his friends before the Zonnebeke action, he was hit in the chest by shell fragments in the Ravebeek Valley near Passchendaele on 11th October 1917 and died instantly. He is buried in the British Military Cemetery at Reninghelst.

5) In Jack's poem to the fallen Tom, he writes of his death and grave 'In France'. Administrators, such as the compilers of 'Officers Died in the Great War', rightly refer to the Western Front as 'France and Flanders', but for many Tommies 'France' sufficed, irrespective of location.

Tom O'Donnell

Jack O'Donnell

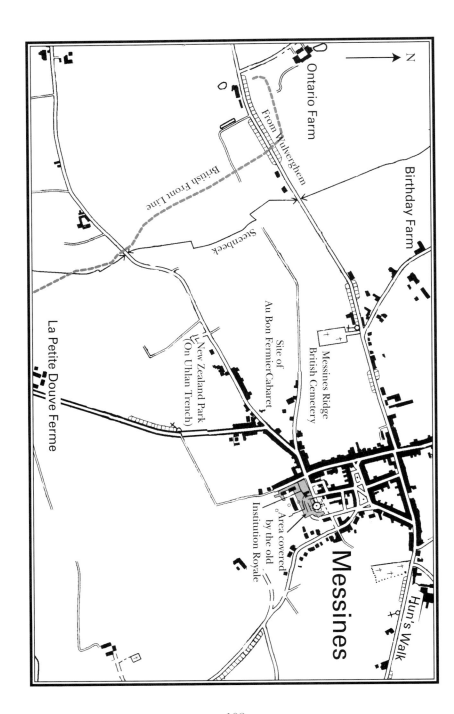

Ontario Farm

From Wulverghem

British Front Line

Birthday Farm

Steenbeck

Au Bon Fermier Cabaret

Site of
New Zealand Park
(On Uhlan Trench)

Messines Ridge
British Cemetery

La Petite Douve Ferme

Area covered
by the old
Institution Royale

Messines

Hun's Walk

N

12
NEW ZEALAND AT THE VILLAGE OF MESSINES
Messines, 7th June 1917

BEFORE BRITISH HIGH COMMAND could consider implementing its major offensive, planned to oust the enemy from Flanders in 1917, it was first essential to clear the strongly-fortified areas on the high ground running from Mount Sorrel, south-east of Ypres, past Wytschaete and Messines to the valley of the River Douve. From this ridge, the Germans commanded unique observation over the whole of the British lines below Ypres, giving them the ability to strike at the flank of any attack originating from within the Ypres Salient. It was to eliminate this threat that High Command conceived what was to be called the Battle of Messines, a battle that, although seemingly unconnected, was an integral part of the Third Battle of Ypres.

The idea of a mining offensive on the Second Army front dated from July 1915, but the proposal to adopt it on a grand scale was only agreed in January, 1916. From that date, deep mining was progressed, resulting in twenty-four mines being tunnelled-in under major German strongpoints along the ridge below Ypres, from Hill 60, south of Zillebeke, to Le Pelerin, east of Ploegsteert Wood. On the day, June 7th 1917, only 19 were triggered, four being outside the front finally chosen for the offensive and one being abandoned due to German counter-mining activity.

As well as mining, preparation for battle above ground went into full swing. Networks of broad- and narrow-gauge railways and trench tramways was expanded; extra ammunition stations, sidings, and forward dumps were sited; new gun emplacements were built; fields of fire were levelled and forward positions selected and prepared for guns to occupy when the ridge was taken. Roads were selected for extension as soon as objectives were gained, with forward *materiel* dumps being set-up for the purpose.[1] Water lines were run well forward from lakes, from catch-pits on the Kemmel Hills, and from sterilising barges on the River Lys. Cable systems were laid, advanced headquarters dugouts excavated, as were signal dugouts, relay posts, regimental aid posts and advanced dressing stations; forward dumps were set-up, approaches were screened, hedgerows in No-Man's Land thinned, portable bridges for spanning rivers prepared and the draining and completion of assembly trenches finalised.

Preparatory bombardment was increased gradually until the end of the month, methodically destroying the enemy's fortifications on the ridge. This caused him to withdraw the bulk of his garrisons to his support-lines, leaving posts on the slopes where only concrete shelters remained intact.

This bombardment increased in intensity in the 10 days preceding the assault with night-firing directed on railway junctions, unloading points, and all known transport halts and approaches. For the last three days, counter-battery bombardment superseded trench bombardment and the enemy's field-guns were largely destroyed or withdrawn to fresh positions in the rear.

The bastion of the enemy defences along the ridge was the village of Messines, on the border of the French-Flemish language-divide in Belgium. This village, atop its steep gradient on the southernmost tip of the ridge, would be the formidable lot of the New Zealand Division, and they would not have the advantage of an exploding mine on their front to distract the enemy facing them, or to help prepare the way for their upward drive.

The division arrived in France in April 1916, having been blooded at Gallipoli. It would make a name for itself on the Somme and earn a reputation for itself second-to-none amongst the outstanding reputations of many divisions that made up the Allied forces. As part of II Anzac Corps, they were to add to this reputation in the forthcoming offensive.

The two German defence systems at the foot and on the crest of the ridge below the village were clearly visible to the New Zealanders from their positions below Hill 63, as were they to the enemy, while atop the ridge, along which the Armentières-Ypres road ran through Messines towards Wytschaete, the skyline was edged with the shell-ruined roofs of the village and the distinctive outline of its church tower. Concrete structures on the slopes abounded - machine-gun nests, observation-posts and dugouts, and a number of strongpoints, each containing two or three machine-guns and a garrison varying from 15 to 40 men.

The New Zealanders' first-stage role was to storm the village, consolidate the trench-lines within their boundaries, establish a series of strongpoints and capture the enemy's guns.

In the late evening of the 6th, advance parties moved to their assembly points. To their right and left lay their sister divisions of II Anzac, the 3rd Australian Division facing the German line from the River Douve to St. Yves, and the 25th Division, holding north of the Wulvergem-Messines road to a point south of Wytschaete.

A thunderstorm had cleared the sultry air, and the night was cool and fresh. German counter-barrage was light, but gas and lachrymatory shells fell with their soft explosions in the New Zealanders' area, especially about Hill 63.

Allied bombardments continued until the moment of attack. A full moon lit the night as patrols out in No-Man's Land examined bridges over the Steenbeek River for any damage, and laid guide-tapes from them over the sluggish stream to the parapets. Others placed duckboards across the New Zealand front trenches as bridges for the troops in the rear. By 3 a.m., these parties were withdrawn to their lines.

The enemy knew an attack was imminent, but did not expect it for some days, and certainly not from below the ground. They decided to relieve their front-line positions accordingly and, on the night of the 6th, these reliefs were still being carried out on the slopes, although in Messines itself they had been completed, and troops of the 40th Division (Saxons) and the 3rd Bavarian Division held the line opposite the New Zealanders.

Zero was 3.10 a.m. The early morning was dark and misty, with dawn just beginning to light the horizon. The tunnellers, with watches and mine-triggering mechanism in hand, awaited the second - and the infantry in their trenches silently fixed bayonets, thinking private thoughts, maybe uttering a silent prayer, but above all, preparing themselves to storm the obstacle-ridden, treacherous upward slope facing them.

Seven seconds before Zero. the two pairs of mines at Factory Farm and Anton's Farm Road, erupted, both sets in the Australian area to the right of the New Zealanders. On their left, and right on time, the Ontario Farm mine blew, as did 14 others all along the ridge to the north.[3]

The mind-bending sound caused by the start-up of the artillery and machine-gun bombardments joined the deafening roar of the mines going up. Ten seconds later, the hillside below Messines was lit by the enemy's white rockets and flares bursting into two green stars, signalling for support and giving observers on Hill 63 a never-to-be-forgotten firework display stretching north as far as their eyes could see. The upward-spurting, jagged, scarlet-red flames and arching flares threw an eery blanket of crimson light over the forms of the New Zealanders clambering over their parapets. Moving forward rapidly they cleared their trenches in seven minutes and swarmed across the Steenbeek.

New Zealand was on its way to Messines.

Two battalions from each brigade, to the south the 1st and 3rd Battalion's, Rifle Brigade, to the north the 1st Canterbury and 1st Otago Battalions of 2nd Brigade, with their machine-gun detachments, covered the 200 yards of No-Man's Land toward the first line of German trenches named Ulna, Ulcer, Uhlan and Oyster Trenches and Supports in record time.

Two platoons of the 1st Rifle Brigade quickly captured La Petite Douve Ferme defences while the main attack crashed through the front-line and rushed the support line, leaving mopping-up parties on the way. At Ulna Support, Corporal H. J. Jeffrey of the 1st Rifles found himself facing an enemy dugout - alone, with a machine-gunner training his weapon on the Australians in the valley below.

He rushed forward, caused the enemy gunner to run back into the dugout and followed him in, throwing bombs and yelling for everyone to surrender. Eight men came out with their hands up. An officer among them made to draw his revolver and Jeffrey lunged at him with his bayonet, but the officer escaped. Another four more men came out with their hands up, and all 12 joined a group of prisoners being escorted to the rear. Jeffrey, who had killed five and wounded another in the dugout, quickly rejoined his platoon.

The 3rd Rifles and 1st Canterbury's in the centre of the line, took their first objectives without problems.

On the left, the 1st Otago overran the German front system, and each of these three battalions sent a party forward to the strongpoints Moulin de l'Hospice and Birthday Farm. They surrounded the former which fell with little resistance, but at Birthday Farm on their extreme left a machine-gun was causing them serious trouble. Bombers started moving from shell-hole to shell-hole to approach it but, before they reached the farm, a shell smashed into it and the occupiers gave up the ghost. The attack moved over the front line trench system so swiftly that the Germans had no time to organise any real resistance. They were bombed in their dugouts or bayonetted within yards of them. Within 16 minutes, the front-system was securely in the hands of the New Zealanders who then moved on up the hill towards the second-line system of trenches, their route pitted with 15-feet deep craters with scarcely a foot of level ground remaining on the shell-torn slope.

Men of the 1st Rifles stormed the trenches on their front, taking 30 prisoners before continuing to their main objective, Ulcer Reserve, about 100 yards further on. Taking fire from behind a hedge while still 200 yards away, they rushed it and bayonetted the Germans in the fortified shell-holes beyond. At Ulcer Reserve, they faced a concrete dugout spouting rifle fire. The riflemen quickly accounted for it, completing their tally of over 70 prisoners and four machine-guns captured.

The 3rd Battalion reached the second-line system and came

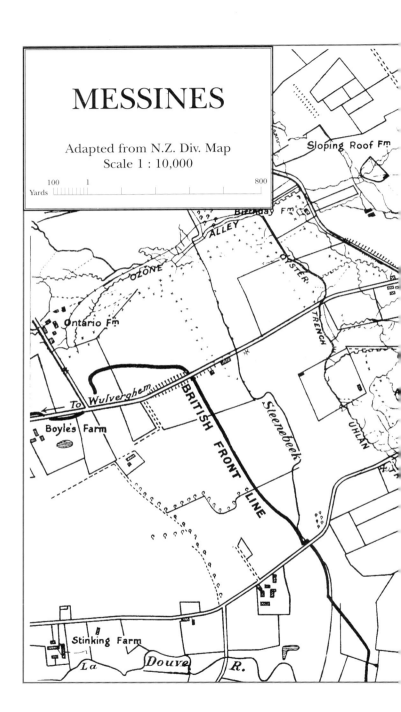

MESSINES

Adapted from N.Z. Div. Map
Scale 1 : 10,000

100   1   800
Yards

Sloping Roof Fm

Birthday Fm

ALLEY

OZONE

OYSTER TRENCH

Ontario Fm

To Wulverghem

BRITISH FRONT LINE

Steenebeek

UHLAN

Boyle's Farm

Stinking Farm

La Douve R.

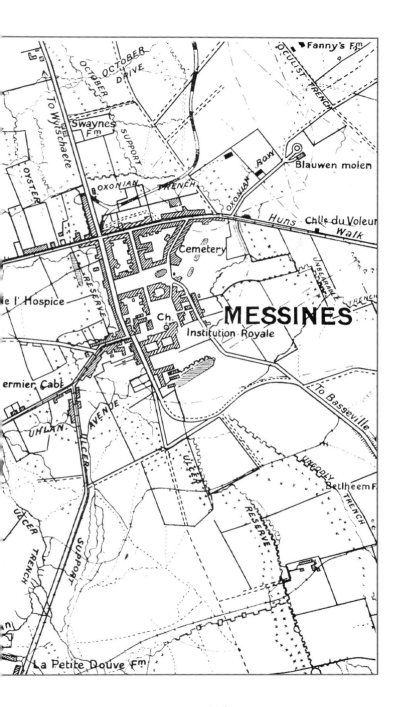

under intense machine-gun fire from a trench edging the village. The line was checked and the battalion was taking casualties. A slightly-wounded Lance-Corporal, Sam Frickleton, shouting for his section to follow, dashed forward through the covering barrage, threw his bombs at the gun crew and bayonetted the survivors. Then, still under shell-fire, he took on another gun 20 yards away, killed the three-man section manning it, then finished-off the remainder of the crew, plus a few others in the dugout for good measure, nine in all, enabling his colleagues to take the trench. Frickleton, later severely wounded, was awarded the Victoria Cross for his efforts.[5]

The 3rd Battalion took nearly 100 prisoners and three machine-guns in the first and second trench systems. Their casualties were 21 killed and 75 wounded, with only nine officers remaining.

Meanwhile, along the farm road dividing the two brigades a 1st Canterbury party captured the strongpoint Au Bon Fermier Cabaret, capturing 17 prisoners and three machine-guns from its cellars. In the further advance, two Lewis gunners, Lance Corporal G. A. Hewitt and Private R. T. Garlick, rushed through their barrage to take on a machine-gun that was causing trouble. The crew made signs of surrender but opened fire as Hewitt and Garlick moved forward, wounding them both. This obviously upset the gunners who, ignoring their wounds, crawled up a sap, killed the six-man crew, rushed the emplacement, took the gun and eleven prisoners - and silenced a gun in the adjoining dugout while they were about it.

The 1st Otago Company took the trench on the right of the battalion's sector and, while doing so, Private C. A. Fitzpatrick rushed a machine-gun, bayonetted five of the crew and captured the gun and the remainder of the crew. 1st Otago captured two field-guns, three trench mortars and nine machine-guns, plus six officers and 150 men. By the evening though, the battalion had lost 11 officers and over 200 men, of whom three officers and 30 men had been killed.

About 4 a.m., the second trench-line fell but 1st Otago was being harassed by machine-guns from the Swayne's Farm strongpoint, north of the village on the Wytschaete road. Fortunately, a tank manoeuvring past a shell-hole, crashed into it caving-in the roof. The garrison of 30 quickly surrendered.

The New Zealanders, having cleaned-up the enemy first and support trenches now gave their full attention to the village itself.

Messines is built on flat ground on the southern tip of the ridge, the ground gradually falling away to the south-east and west. These slopes were covered with barbed-wire as part of the defences. Heavily-wired trenches north, north-east and west of it completed the outlying defence-line with five concrete dugouts commanding the lines of streets within. These dugouts were the crux of the inner defences, each a self-contained strongpoint, with the cellars of the 200-odd houses they commanded converted into concrete shelters, to be used as offices, telephone exchanges, general accommodation and reserve billets.

The 4th Rifles and 2nd Canterburys, leap-frogging through their compatriot battalions, attacked defences to the north, south and east. The 2nd Canterburys on the left took Oxonian Trench which ran from the Wytschaete road to Hun's Walk, the main communication line servicing Messines from the east, capturing 50 prisoners. They also took a trench-line east of the village, extending south of Hun's Walk to Unbearable Trench, a 'switch' between Messines and the Oosttaverne Line, the overall objective of the offensive in this sector of the line. Later they overran October Support trench on their left beyond the road to Wytschaete, north of the village. The 4th Rifles took the southern half of the village and the trenches that completed its encirclement to the south and south-west, back to the second-line system.

The main assault poured into the dust-filled, shell-battered, smoking village where they were sniped and bombed from doorways and windows, from behind walls and from any position that gave a minimum of cover to the enemy. Machine-gun fire was blasting at them from all sides and they were taking casualties. Nevertheless, the resistance was disorganised, so fast and furious had been the New Zealanders' progress. They soon overcame the main pockets of resistance, five machine-guns were captured before they could be brought into action, five were attacked on the run and overcome and two others, firing across the village square, were taken-out with rifle grenades. Yet another, firing from a position in a dressing station, was attacked by a party led by Private F. White, 2nd Canterburys who captured the gun after killing all the crew. Earlier that morning, he had taken 18 prisoners while clearing an enemy dugout and, in another part of the village, killed an enemy sniper who was making a nuisance of himself. After silencing the gun in the dressing station, he turned his attention to another which was becoming troublesome, rushed it, bayonetted five of the crew and brought back the sixth - with the gun. Wounded at the end of the day, he was awarded the D.C.M. Apart from killing Germans, Private White took pride in being the company barber during quieter times and, following his exploits in the village on 7th June, he no doubt became a barber with a reputation and would be treated with a great deal of deference by his future customers.

Meanwhile, cellars were being cleared with bomb and bayonet or, if the occupants chose to put up a fight, by light mortars. The German commanding officer, with his complete staff, were captured in a large dugout under the Institution Royale, a Roman Catholic Orphanage in better times.

The 4th Rifles had captured a field-gun, three machine-guns and over 60 prisoners. The 2nd Canterburys, facing larger numbers, captured more prisoners, plus 20 machine-guns, two trench mortars, three anti-tank guns and four searchlights.

Thus the village of Messines, if not cleared completely in its northern half, now belonged, for all intents and purposes, to the New Zealand infantry. In a little under two hours of hard, brutal fighting, overcoming what had been accepted as impregnable defences on a steep, upward slope, culminating in the hazardous environment of house-to-house and street-fighting inside an enemy fortress, the men of New Zealand had triumphed - and exactly to the scheduled time of 5 a.m. Official confirmation of the capture reached Divisional Headquarters at 7 a.m. The II Anzac action on this part of the ridge was an unqualified success with its

25th Division to the left and the 3rd Australian Division to the right experiencing equal success over a mine-stunned, but hard fighting enemy. From Hill 60 down to the St. Yves Ridge, the results of the action were expounded in a similar vein

The New Zealanders had done the job in their sector. They did it well and right on schedule. The final objective for the the New Zealand Division, the Black Line further over the ridge, would be reached and overcome later. But this was the work-load of the New Zealand 1st Brigade who would now play its part and complete the second stage of the action.

The overall offensive, called the Battle of Messines, was not finished by a long stroke, but the battle of the village of Messines was. In enemy hands since 1914, this once impregnable bastion now belonged to the New Zealand infantry.

From the germ of the idea in 1915 until its implementation in June of 1917, the Staff work preceding the opening of the Messines Offensive had surpassed excellence. Every detail had been well-planned, practised and brilliantly put into action, and every man involved had a carefully rehearsed task, knowing exactly what was expected of him. The bombardments, before and during the battle, were an exercise in pure excellence, and praise was poured upon the artillerymen from all quarters - even the infantry had contributed much to this praise, and to have prompted such a reaction from the infantry was, in itself, a sure sign that the bombardments must have neared perfection! However, as one Brigadier recorded:

> I attribute our success to the careful and methodical preparations which were made during the weeks preceding the attack, but above all I attribute it to the magnificent leading of all officers and non-commissioned officers and to the incomparable bravery of our men.

What better words could describe the achievement of those New Zealanders. They would continue to prove their worth on the battlefields of Europe, and would, sadly, leave many of their compatriots behind in the clusters of military cemeteries along the old Western Front when the time came for them to return to their home islands edging the Pacific Ocean.

Notes:

1. After 7th June, roads were extended with great rapidity to Messines, Wytschaete, and Oosttaverne, across country so completely destroyed by shell fire that it was difficult to trace where the original road had run.

2. New sectors in the area were christened with names such as Otira, Otago and Auckland Trenches, in memory of the New Zealanders' homes adding to those already bearing names reminiscent of former Canadian occupation. This mixture of names reflected the co-operation and sacrifice of two widely separated Dominions in support of the British cause.

3. The gallery for the Ontario Farm mine, started on 28th January 1917, was lost after 100 yards due to ground complications. This delay caused the final laying of the mine to fall short of its objective, although still under the German line. It was finalised and charged just one day before the offensive.

4. The New Zealand Division assault battalions were the New Zealand Rifle Brigade - 1st, 2nd, 3rd and 4th Rifle Battalions and the 2nd New Zealand Infantry Brigade - 2nd Battalions of the Auckland Canterbury, Otago and Wellington Regiments. The 1st New Zealand Infantry Brigade, who passed through the assaulting brigades following the capture of Messines, was made-up of the 1st Battalions of the Auckland, Canterbury, Otago and Wellington Regiments.

5. The German trench names began with the letter of the map square in which they were located. The New Zealand attack fell mainly in the square U and partly in the square O and the trenches of the front-line system (Blue Line) were named, from south to north Ulna, Ulcer, Uhlan and Oyster Trenches and Supports.

6. The Institution Royale was formerly a Roman Catholic orphanage for girls. The Mother Superior had earlier cheerfully agreed to watch it under bombardment from behind the British lines. The area it covered is today an open space forming a small square in front of the church, open tree-lined walks to one side of it and the ground upon which some of the post-war dwellings were built. The church itself was just a small part of the overall building complex.

7. L/Cpl. Samuel Frickleton's citation (*London Gazette*, 2nd August 1917) read: *No. 6/2133, Samuel Frickleton, L.Corpl. 3rd Battn. New Zealand Infantry. For most conspicuous bravery and determination when with attacking troops which came under heavy fire and were checked. Although slightly wounded, Corpl. Frickleton dashed forward at the head of his section, pushed into our barrage, and personally destroyed with bombs an enemy machine-gun and crew which was causing heavy casualties. He then attacked a second gun, killing the whole of the crew of twelve. By the destruction of these two guns, he undoubtedly saved his own and other units from very severe casualties, and his magnificent courage and gallantry ensured the capture of the objective. During the consolidation of this position he received a second severe wound. He set throughout a great example of heroism.*

The upward slope facing the New Zealand infantry from the centre of their jumping-off line on 7th June 1917 as it is today. The white obelisk of the New Zealand Park Memorial stands on part of the lower flat ground that once was part of the Oyster-Uhlan trench first-line system. The distinctive church tower on the crest identifies the area where was situated the Institution Royale, with the German Command Headquarters in its cellars.

121

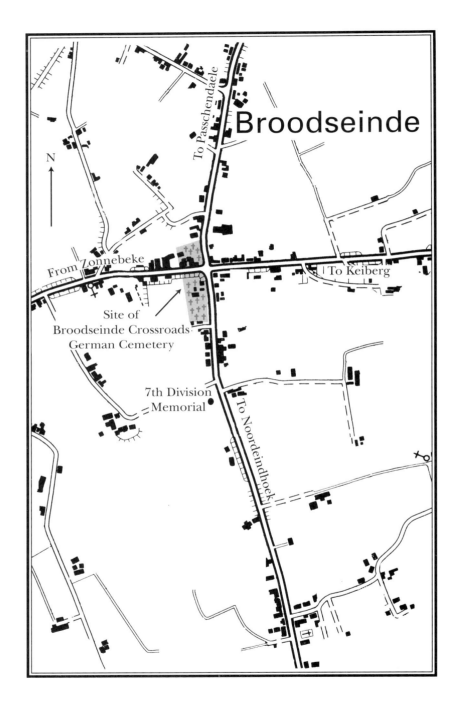

Broodseinde

N

To Passchendaele

From Zonnebeke

To Keiberg

Site of
Broodseinde Crossroads
German Cemetery

7th Division
Memorial

To Noordeindhoek

13

RECONCILIATION AT BROODSEINDE
Broodseinde Crossroads German Cemetery, 1931

HATE IS AN EMOTION that does not sit easily with the Anglo-Saxon character. Not for him the unrelenting hatred for an enemy once the heat of battle has subsided. A new mood takes over, born from the realisation that his enemy had endured the same agonies. This could help explain the Christmas Truce of 1914 south of Ypres. With the First Battle of Ypres hardly settled, men of the British Expeditionary Force clambered from behind their breastworks, ventured into the mist and hoar frost of No-Man's Land, and met with their Saxon cousins to celebrate the coming of the Prince of Peace. They took the opportunity to bury the dead from earlier actions, talked of happier times, exchanged gifts and pleasantries and played each other in a game of football. They then resumed the pressing business of conducting war against each other.

The Great War resulted in an awesome loss of life for both sides, but it was scattered throughout with acts of compassion displaying a nobility of spirit which allowed one combatant to retain a vestige of respect and understanding for the other. This mutual respect continued into the immediate post-war years when the battlefields were being reclaimed.

In and around the confines of the old Salient were to be found over a thousand burial plots of both sides. They varied in size from a couple of lonely graves tucked away in the corner of a churchyard to many thousands in vast areas where their gathering together later formed the basis of the larger cemeteries such as those at Tyne Cot and Lijssenthoek.

The German concentration of graves did not reach its zenith until the 1930s with cemeteries sited at Menin with 48,000 graves, Langemarck with 44,000, Vladso with 26,000 and Hooglede with 9,000, a total of 127,000 in all.

One of their cemeteries, containing nearly 1,000 graves, once straddled the Broodseinde Crossroads on the ridge near the village of Zonnebeke. It had developed after the fighting had receded following the early battles of 1914-1916. During the summer of 1917 when the Passchendaele fighting was at its height, this cemetery became a battleground itself as infantry of the Australian 2nd Division stormed the Broodseinde Ridge to secure the vital crossroads.

In the late 1920s as the people returned to the battered Salient to work their fields and come to terms with the peace, it was

The German cemetery at Broodseinde crossroads with the church steeple at Zonnebeke visible in the background.

common to see parties of ex-servicemen from both sides wandering the old battlegrounds like lost souls, seeking-out the graves of their comrades. This was before mass touring had become popular, when only family and close friends would make the Pilgrimage.

Flanders was at peace again and its fields no longer reverberated to the clamour of machine-gun fire, or the roar of heavy cannon, but they were still to see some strange scenes. One of them began to unfold on the morning of Whit Sunday 1931. Enemies were about to gather together again as they did once before in the Christmas Truce of 1914, although now 'old enemies' would better describe the participants.

Acts of reconciliation in the German Cemetery at Broodseinde and the British Cemetery at Tyne Cot were developing as instanced by the following account published in the *Ypres Times*

The Broodseinde crossroads today, without the German graves, but with the church steeple at Zonnebeke visible in the background

in January, 1932 by Sergeant F. J. Lineton, 6th Battalion, King's Shropshire Light Infantry, 20th Light Division:

On Whit-Sunday morning, 1931, the sun shone brightly through the historic streets of Ypres as my chum and I bent our steps towards Skindle's Hotel, near the railway station, where breakfast awaited us.

And then a strange sight met our gaze, for out of the station they poured, a large party of our late enemies. These were men to whom, for four weary years of agony and bloody sweat, we barred the road to Ypres. "They shall not pass," that was our watchword and on roads and fields of sacrifice we stood until the peace.

Eagerly we studied the faces of these men as they gazed curiously back at the new city which had sprung up from the ashes of the old Ypres. One of them carried a wreath, and that emblem of homage told the object of their pilgrimage. They had come back to pay tribute to old comrades who had laid down their lives in an enemy country, men who had died for the Fatherland in a cause they believed to be just. It was just that fact which drew us close to them in spirit, for we too had come back to pay homage to brave comrades who had died for the Motherland.

I greeted the man who carried the wreath, with an English "Good morning." A friendly smile suffused the face of this one time enemy as he returned my greeting and somehow I knew immediately that I had met a natural gentleman of whose friendship I should be proud.

Asking their destination and intentions I received a reply that they were to hold a memorial ceremony in Broodseinde German Cemetery and afterwards they were to tour the Salient. Then he surprised me with a very pressing invitation; he and his friends would be pleased to offer seats in their buses to me and my comrades, in all the circumstances a generous invitation. Instinctively, they seemed to know that we were one with them in their desire to perpetuate the memory of brave men who had died on the battlefields of Flanders. I explained our inability to spend the day with them due to other arrangements, but said we would hire a car and join them at Broodseinde and Tyne Cot.

Soon we were speeding to Broodseinde between bus loads of German ex-servicemen, my party now numbering four. Arriving at the German Cemetery, we removed our hats as we entered.

Our gesture of reverence for the resting-place of our late enemies seemed to be much appreciated by our new friends.

A German ex-officer, wearing the Iron Cross, mounted a temporary pulpit and made a very earnest speech, or so it seemed to his compatriots. We learned later that this officer had been wounded, while serving in the Salient, no less than five times. This was followed by an old comrades song and a ceremony of laying the wreath on one of the rude Trees of Calvary which border the west side of the cemetery.

After the ceremony I again sought my English-speaking friend and regretfully he said that they might not have time to visit Tyne Cot, but if possible they would do so. He then asked me if I would correspond with him and we exchanged addresses. Then with many hearty handshakes we left them and took the road to Tyne Cot.

We had been in the cemetery for five minutes when I saw the German party arriving. Reverently, with heads bared, they entered the gate; I was deeply moved at their reverent attitude, it made one marvel at the madness of the dark war years. We met them at a spot where two German soldiers lay buried, their graves carefully tended and covered with lovely flowers by British gardeners. They seemed to be very interested and deeply appreciative of the work of our great-hearted caretakers.

I asked one of my friends to make a speech of welcome to our new friends. He did not do so but asked the English-speaking German to pass on our appreciation and welcome. He quickly responded by standing on the steps of the Stone of Remembrance and addressing his comrades, and finally, called for a two minutes' silent homage to our dead. Standing close to me a burly Teuton wept.

What a wonderful sight; surely around us field grey and khaki, though unseen, stood hand in hand.

Walking back to the gates our friend who had called for the silence said "Your cemeteries are very beautiful; they are lovely and much nicer than ours." What a tribute to the Britisher's reverence for dead comrades.

Once again we stood on one of the Flanders' roads of memory and sorrow, the hands of one-time enemies met in a firm grip, a grip which meant the beginning of an understanding friendship, a grip which expressed sincere regret for the mistakes and misunderstanding which a few years back had sent two mighty empires flying at each others throats. Here on this very soil had we striven to kill each other. In Tyne Cot lay 12,000 of our dead, evidence of the titanic struggle.

Hard by the erstwhile fields of death lay tilled and smiling in the early summer sunshine. "Oh God! For the sake of millions of dead, let us keep this peace, let us strive for understanding, that way lies peace." Now, may I make a suggestion to Ypres Leaguers, on which I should welcome observations. Could we do our bit for peace by arranging at Easter, Whitsuntide, or August, a meeting between our members and this German ex-service organisation to take place in the Salient.

We could mix freely together for a programme of tours, with, say, a commemoration ceremony at the Menin Gate and possibly one at Broodseinde German Cemetery.[1] It would give a wonderful opportunity for the exchange of experiences and impressions from both sides of No Man's Land, but best of all it would help the cause of peace and for that a million Britishers gave their lives.

The aspirations of our Ypres League friend were not realised and later, in the 1930s, war-clouds once again blurred the horizon and gun-fire was heard again around Ypres with the British defending the Comines Canal line in May 1940, attempting to keep open the Dunkirk escape route for yet another British Expeditionary Force under attack by the same enemy. Ypres was again suffering the tribulations of war, a war conducted by the same adversaries as in the 1914-18 conflict.

The Broodseinde Crossroads saw the last of the invader when, in September 1944 he was chased over the ridge top, away from Ypres, by a Polish armoured column.

What were the thoughts of those old soldiers from the opposing armies when, only eight years after their reconciliation at Broodseinde in the early 1930s, their kin were again at war with each other. So much for their aspirations of keeping peace for the sake of the millions who died in the Great War.

Notes:

1 The bodies of the fallen in the German Military Cemetery at Broodseinde Crossroads were exhumed in the middle of 1952 and re-buried at the main German concentration area at Langemarck.

German and British veterans of the 1914-18 conflict honour the German dead at the Broodseinde German Cemetery at the Broodseinde crossroads, Whitsun 1931

BIBLIOGRAPHY

Canada in Flanders. Lord Beaverbrook. Hodder & Stoughton, 1917.
War Diary of the 1st Life Guards, First Year 1914-1915.
Diary kept by Captain the Hon. E. H. Wyndham.
Charles Sackville Pelham Lord Worsley.
An Appreciation by his father. Roffey & Clarke Croydon, 1924.
German Divisions, 1914-1918. Records of the Intelligence section
of the General Staff, American Expeditionary Forces, Chaumont,
France, 1919. Washington Government Printing Office, 1920.
Gheluvelt, 31st October 1914. Worcestershire County Council
Stationery Dept. (1915). IMCC Ltd., London, 1998.
Hawker V.C. Tyrrel M. Hawker. Mitre Press, London, 1965.
History of the London Rifle Brigade 1895-1919.
Constable & Co Ltd., London, 1921.
Newsletter of the Friends of St. George's Memorial Church.
Researched by S. Arnold, Ypres 1995.
Over There with O'Ryan's Roughnecks.
W. F. Clarke. Superior Publishing Co., Seattle, U.S.A., 1996.
Officers Died in the Great War 1914-1919.
His Majesty's Stationery Office, 1919.
*Official History of the Canadian Forces in the Great war, 1914-19,
Vol. I. - Aug. 1914-Sept. 1915.*
Ministry of National Defence. J. O. Patenaude. I.S.O. 1938.
*Official History of New Zealand's Effort in the Great War, Vol. II.,
France.* Col. H. Stewart, C.M.G., D.S.O., M.C. Whitcombe and Tombs
Limited, New Zealand, 1921.
*Official History of the War, Military Operations, France and Belgium
1915, Vol. I.* Macmillan & Co., 1927.
*Regimental Records of the Royal Welch Fusilers (23rd Regiment),
Vol. III., 1914-1918, France and Flanders.* Major C. H. Dudley-Ward
D.S.O., M.C. Foster Groom & Co. Ltd., London, 1928.
Tank Warfare. F. Mitchell M.C. Thomas Nelson and Sons Ltd.
The Battle Book of Ypres. Beatrix Brice/Lieut.-General Sir William
Pulteney, K.C.B. etc. John Murray, London, 1927.
The History of the Rifle Brigade in the War of 1914-18.
Reginald Berkeley M.C. Rifle Brigade Club, London 1927.
The History of the Second Division, Vol. I. 1914-1916.
Everard Wyrall. Thomas Nelson and Sons Ltd., 1921.

The King's Regiment (Liverpool) 1914 - 1918.
Everard Wyrall. Edward Arnold & Co., London, 1935.
The Orange, Green and and Khaki, Irish Regiments 1914-1918.
Tom Johnston. Gill and Macmillan, Dublin, 1992.
The Story of the Household Cavalry. Captain Sir George Arthur
Bart. William Heinemman Ltd., London, 1926.
The Tanks, The History of the Royal Tank Regiment Vol. I.
Captain B. H. Liddell Hart. Cassell, London, 1959.
The V.C. and D.S.O. Sir O'Moore Creagh, V.C., G.C.S.I. and
E. M. Humphris. The Standard Art Book Co. Ltd., 1924.
The Welsh at Ypres, October 31st 1914.
Swansea Mabinogion Society (1918). IMCC Ltd., London, 1998.
The Worcestershire Regiment in the Great War. Capt. H. FitzM.
Stacke M.C. G. T. Cheshire & Sons Ltd., Kidderminster, 1928.
Ypres, 1914.
German General Staff. Constable & Co Ltd., London 1919.
Ypres-Outpost of the Channel Ports.
Beatrix Brice. Ypres League/John Murray, London, 1929.
Ypres Times. 1931.
Ypres Times. 1923.
Private Papers: Mr P. W. Leigh
                  Mr & Mrs Joseph O'Donnell
                  Jack Patten
                  Tony Spagnoly
                  Ted Smith

INDEX

The CAMEOS OF THE WESTERN FRONT
1914-1918

The *Cameos of the Western Front* series by Tony Spagnoly and Ted Smith is directed at giving the Great War enthusiast a deeper insight into the minor actions of the Great War and the men involved in them. Developed as a collection of short, colourful pen-pictures, or cameos, of individuals, their units and almost forgotten episodes in which they were involved in the Ypres Salient, it covers subjects and specific areas often neglected by writers and historians of the 1914-1918 conflict. The series will add much detail of interest and information to students of the Great War and, to those who visit the battlefields of the old Western Front, will act as an excellent companion and supplement to any guide the visitor may be using.

A Walk Round Plugstreet, their third book was originally intended to be a group of short stories. The authors decided that Plugstreet merited a production in its own right as did their first book, *The Anatomy of a Raid, Australia at Broodseinde, October 1917*, which had begun life as a short, cameo-style story. They will continue to produce the *Cameos of the Western Front* series on the Ypres sector of the Western Front, then gradually move southward down the old front-line until they reach the Somme.

Both authors were sea cadets, both are ex-Royal Navy and Londoners, and both lived in the same area for years before meeting each other on the battlefields of northern France. Born in 1928, Tony Spagnoly served in destroyers in the Far East and, on leaving the service, spent his professional life in the engineering and electronic industries. His deep interest in the Great War resulted in many research projects on the old battlefields of Flanders and Picardy.

Ted Smith, born in 1936, moved to Paris in 1966 and then to Brussels in 1967 where he opened his own business, only returning to London in 1988. When he was not travelling with his job in international advertising and marketing, he spent most of his spare time on the battlefields of Belgium and France.

The Salient Points series of books is published by
LEO COOPER
an imprint of
Pen & Sword Books Limited,
47 Church Street, Barnsley,
South Yorkshire, S70 2 BR

Telephone: 01226 734222/734555 Fax: 01226 734438
E mail: p&sword@barnsley-chronicle.co.uk
World Wide Web site: http://www.yorkshire-web.co.uk/ps/
DX:2501 Barnsley 2

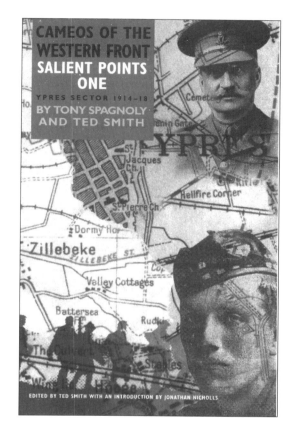

Cameos of the Western Front
SALIENT POINTS ONE
Ypres Sector, 1914-1918

This book is directed at giving the Great War battlefield visitor a deeper insight into some of the activities and minor actions of the war. It takes a close and detailed look at individuals and events, bringing to life the characters and types of men who were involved. Made up of a collection of short, colourful pen-pictures, or cameos of individuals, their units and almost forgotten episodes in which they were involved.

Size 216x135cm, extent, 178 pages
Price: £9.95
ISBN 085052 319 2

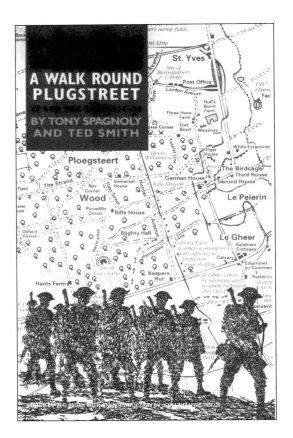

Cameos of the Western Front
A WALK ROUND PLUGSTREET
Ypres Sector, 1914-1918

This book highlights a multitude of little-known actions, places of interest and the activities of the men who served in the Ploegsteert, or Plugstreet sector, as it was known to the troops during the Great War. Much has been written of Plugstreet's links with Bruce Bairnsfather's 'Old Bill' but little has been documented of its importance during the early and mid-stages of the war. This book brings to life the Plugstreet area of the Western Front, in which most regiments of the British and Comonwealth armies served.

Size 216x135cm, extent, 178 pages
Price: £9.95
ISBN 085052 570 5